Dr Lin Berwick MBE is a writer, lecturer, broadcaster and freelance journalist, despite being totally blind, having Cerebral Palsy Quadriplegia, partial deafness and being a permanent wheelchair user. She has previously published five books. She was cared for by her mother, Alma, and her father, George, until she met and married her husband, Ralph, who loved and cared for her for almost twenty-five years until he died. Lin's passion is classical music—she loves going to concerts, socialising with friends and eating out. Lin has recently been appointed the first Ambassador to The National Bobath Cerebral Palsy Centre.

I dedicate this book to all of my carers who support me brilliantly in my daily life. I love and care about all of them and wish them to know how deeply grateful I am to each and every one of them. This book is dedicated to all of my unsung heroes and I wish to thank them from the bottom of my heart for all they do and for all that they are. God bless and thank you

Dr Lin Berwick (MBE)

GOD AND OUR
DIRTY SOCKS

To Dr Alison Cook,

*I hope you will enjoy
the pages of my new book.
With best wishes.*

Lin Berwick

AUSTIN MACAULEY PUBLISHERS®

LONDON • CAMBRIDGE • NEW YORK • SHARJAH

A CIP catalogue record for this title is available from the British Library.

ISBN 9781035867233 (Paperback)
ISBN 9781035867240 (ePub e-book)

www.austinmacauley.com

First Published 2024
Austin Macauley Publishers Ltd®
1 Canada Square
Canary Wharf
London
E14 5AA

I would like to acknowledge the following individuals who have assisted me greatly with the production of my 6th book, titled "God and Our Dirty Socks." Firstly, thanks should go to all the staff at Austin Macauley Publishers for their invaluable help and support in bringing this book to fruition. I am deeply grateful to all of them and trust that my 7th book will appear shortly.

I would also like to acknowledge my dear friend Jonquil Johnson, who supported me financially to cover my contribution to Austin Macauley. I am profoundly grateful for her encouragement and support throughout the writing of this book.

Special thanks to Mr. Stephen Karl Cottage, my former personal assistant funded by Access to Work, for his assistance with the final editing of this text. And last but not least, I want to acknowledge my new personal assistant, Emma Holdsworth, who has taken over from Stephen Cottage. I am confident that together we will continue to produce books and articles that will be enjoyed by my readers. I hope you will all enjoy this new book. I see it as the kind of bedside table book that readers can turn to for inspiration or a restful night.

God bless you all, Dr Lin Berwick MBE

Table of Contents

Introduction

This is a book of meditations on the theme of the Family. I've a wealth of material to write about. *God and Our Dirty Socks* is about the mishmash of family life, some of which may be loving and caring, some of which may be contentious. *God and Our Dirty Socks* is, if you like, washing our dirty laundry in public—an open door on family life, which we have been privileged to share.

I suppose, on such a subject as the family, one would have much to say; however, I have tried to give an overall representation of what I think are the subjects that regularly come up. Whilst it's important to be positive, I've always tried to write these themes looking at both sides of the coin and I hope, through the writing of this text, you'll feel that I've been mindful of those readers who didn't have a good family life experience.

This realisation used to come to me strongly when I prepared services, as a Methodist local preacher, for Mothering Sunday. Not all people in the congregation had a good experience of mothers—some may not have had a mother at all, others may not have been married, or experienced close family life. With that thought firmly fixed in my mind, I've tried to be fair and balanced in my writing. I hope that you'll be able to turn up some of the issues and recognise them for yourself. Some of the themes of the meditations, I'm sure, you'll be experiencing at this very moment and others will certainly be in your scope of experience for the future.

Whether you have experienced them personally, or not, I trust that you'll be able to identify with them, and find some spiritual solace in what I'm trying to say. Of course, I know that relationships within families are complex; they can be, on the one hand loving, but on the other, hateful or very difficult. As a counsellor, with more than thirty years' experience, I've been privileged to share in many aspects of family life and trauma with the clients that I've seen.

In that situation, the role of the counsellor is to be a reflective mirror and help the client to see the opposing view, it's not to be judgemental or directive but to help them see another viewpoint. Therefore, I've a wealth of material on which to draw. It's the one advantage counsellors have, they're able to listen to many scenarios on a similar theme. Although I can't be specific, I will endeavour to explore many issues in a creative way.

For many, the fact that they have had to seek the help of a counsellor is viewed as failure. I would like to turn this notion on its head and say that to seek counselling is actually success, because the person recognises that they have a problem and they have the desire to seek help from somebody who is not emotionally involved, and who can offer another point of view. It is important that those seeking counselling give the counsellor the opportunity to do their work—a one hour session is not going to put right what may be several years of inappropriate behaviour within their relationship. I would suggest that those seeking counselling, should budget for a minimum of six sessions. If the rapport between you and the counsellor is good, then stay with it and make a commitment to create change—even if it hits your pocket!

All I can try to do is strike a middle ground and hope that the thoughts and prayers hold some meaning for you.

Good luck and God bless
Dr Lin Berwick MBE

Relationships and Courtship

If we start from the premise that every human being is unique, and as such deserves our respect and dignity, then the way we'll approach a newfound friendship, subsequently a courtship, will be different than if we believe that that person is only there for us to have a good time with. There's nothing wrong with having a good time, if that is the basis on which the friendship is founded. Where it goes awry is when one person thinks that the relationship has more potential in it for a long-term future than the other. Our body is something to be valued, something that should be cherished, not only by ourselves, but by another person. If we only see our body as a vehicle for sexual arousal, then we have missed out on the precious gift given to us by God, the gift of life itself. It's what we do with that life and how we treat others that really matters.

Men will say that you can never understand the mind of a woman. Women will say that men are a breed apart. Both descriptions are true. For a relationship to work, there has to be a middle ground and a meeting of minds and hearts.

One of the best aspects of friendship and courtship is discovering one another, by that, I don't just mean sexual discovery—I mean what makes a person tick. Are they compassionate and sensitive, and thereby loving? Look at any star sign in a magazine and you'll quickly work out the emotional traits of each. For the record, I'm Pisces, and I think

I'm a bit of an old romantic at heart, and a dreamer, I suppose that's what writers are, they think most of the time and eventually spill out their thoughts on paper.

I hope that what I write is relevant, but I know you'll take away from it whatever you wish, and disregard the parts that don't hold meaning for you. Relationships are like that, we take from them the bits that are important and disregard the rest. But unlike a well-worn suit, or a comfortable pair of shoes, we have to meet people where they are, we can't set out to change them. After all, if that's our intention then why did we form a relationship with them in the first place? We have to start from the premise of total acceptance, then, if there are issues that we grapple with in our emotions, this is the basis upon which we try to create change, not by forcing our opinions, but by loving the person, and finding a meeting of minds through loving acceptance.

That can only happen when time is given in this regard. But when couples use each other, just for the purpose of sexual gratification, that is when it has a horrible habit of going wrong—no relationship will last on this basis. For when you think about the sexual side of any relationship, it's a very small part of our daily existence, I'm not denigrating its importance, but what we share in intimately should be an extension of loving feelings for that person, which has built in our heart over time.

It's difficult to keep those feelings in check, and wait until we are sure of ourselves and of the other person. This is two-way traffic. It's also a time for mutual respect and admiration of one another. After all, if we can't rejoice and delight in another human being at that point in our life, when can we? Respect and admiration doesn't come in less than twenty-four hours, it comes over time, and grows. The finding of true love is like the nurturing of a plant. The first time you see it you're amazed by its potential, and thrilled by its blossoming, but unless it's watered, nurtured, fed properly, and put in the right kind of soil, so that it can put down roots and remain there, it will fade away.

The analogy of a plant and its care is a good one for us, because we're like that beautiful plant. We need the right words said, we need loving tender care, we need to feel good about ourselves, and, more importantly, we need to feel safe and firmly rooted in the relationship before we can express ourselves in the kind of abandonment and carefree way that we all hope for.

A thought:

We want our courtship to be a memorable affair. Sometimes we have to own that it doesn't always work out, however hard we might try, we have to learn that if you have to work so hard, almost like kicking a door in, then this relationship may not be for you. A relationship that works is one where you feel wholly comfortable, wholly at peace, and restful in the other person's presence. Rather like that good old comfortable pair of shoes or slippers, you'll know when it's right, and you'll know when letting your heart rule your head is appropriate.

Don't be afraid of it, go with it and enjoy it.

A prayer:

Lord, it's an exciting time when a couple start out on a new relationship, especially when they only have eyes for each other. That sense of utter obliviousness about the world around them is wonderful, would that sense of wonderment continue. Lord, help them to seek out and know the good qualities in one another. Help them to give of their best, help them to truly value the other person, and let there be a mutual admiration between them. Lord, I pray that this special relationship will not be spoilt by bickering and point-scoring, that if it doesn't gel between them, that they amicably separate, before they harm one another emotionally.

Lord, let the two people concerned choose each other wisely and lovingly, and may it be a time of long-lasting growth and blessings between them.

Wedding Day

There's nothing more glorious than when two people realise that they want to spend the rest of their lives together. That may be a simple statement to make, but the implications behind it are truly tremendous. It's so easy to get caught up in all the preparation for the great day and forget what it's really all about.

Weddings are becoming increasingly more expensive, and whilst we want a memorable occasion, it isn't necessary to break the bank to do it. The wedding vows that we make before God are incredibly important, and ought to be taken very seriously. This is a public pronouncement of the fact that a couple want to be together, and make their commitment to each other before God.

The day should be one that you will remember and treasure for the rest of your life, something that, hopefully, you will tell your children about. All too often, the church is seen by some to be there for marriages, baptisms and funerals, rather than an essential part of a couple's life. No one can tell somebody how to live, or what to do, but a marriage is all the more special when there are three in it, husband, wife, and God. This is the start of a journey—a journey where the sat-nav isn't telling you where to go, and a journey of discovery, trials, tribulations, and pitfalls along the way. But hopefully, it's a journey that will cement the vows that you make together, which will stand you in good stead in times of trouble.

When everything is plain sailing, it's easy, but when the road gets tough, that's when you find out how much you truly love each other. It doesn't have to be the big things in life that create happiness, ask many people who have won the lottery, and a huge number of them will tell you that it doesn't bring happiness, it brings plenty of complications! Happiness comes with the little things, often the things that cost nothing in financial terms, but it's those that will bring lasting happiness and memories.

On your wedding day, it's the first step down that very delightful road—hopefully, you'll enjoy the walk and rejoice in what's around you.

A thought:

A newly married couple will only have eyes for each other, but they'll also need family and friends to be supportive and loving. The wife will need her mother or a good friend, who can give her friendly advice and the husband will need a friendly ear, even if it's from his workmates as they share a drink at the bar. It's all too easy to be critical. What we should be doing, is rejoicing in the couple's success, and be happy for them, being there for them when they need friendly support, but not being too ready to give your advice— especially if you're a parent, and not to be too offended if they don't take it. The couple have to be allowed to find their own way—it may just be a different way from that of their parents, but life progresses, and moves on.

A prayer:

Lord, on their wedding day, let them really feel that they have come together—a union in every sense of the word—spiritually, emotionally, and physically. Let them be patient with one another, discovering all the little things—some may be wonderful, others irritating, but let it be a time of laughter, rejoicing, and happiness. Let there be good communication between the couple, each one respecting the other. Let this marriage give each of them a sense of mutual admiration for each other. Love is like a plant, if it's not nurtured, touched lovingly and tenderly, it won't survive, so help them to see each other as something precious and worth nurturing, and may they have a long, happy and fulfilled life together.

Setting Up Home

It's quite an exciting time when you decide to look for a property, which will be the first place where you'll put down roots together, a firm foundation for your future life. It's exciting and, at the same time, daunting to go with an estate agent to look around a property. It can be difficult to look at someone else's home and visualise how it'll be when you own it, but that's the glorious challenge. Atmosphere is crucial when you walk around a property, the vibes have to be right, and it's something that's instinctual, you'll feel it instantly.

So many couples, when they're newly-wed, start out with all the things that it took our parents years to save up for, so they don't always appreciate how much better it is to pull together as a couple, and work for the things that they want to have in their home. There's a real feeling of excitement when you finally have enough money to buy the new lounge carpet, for example, and decorate. It's the planning that makes the marriage, with all of the expectancy, hopes and dreams coming to fruition. That's truly wonderful and it makes a marriage complete—and a couple complete. However, it can also be a time of conflict. You may have a real strong difference of opinion concerning decor, which can only be resolved by finding an acceptable middle ground.

It's a time when ground rules are set down, the sharing of household tasks, the domesticity of everyday life, which could become humdrum if you let it. Nevertheless, it can also be a time when mutual respect and appreciation of one another really comes to the fore, a sense in which you each recognise that to do a job well, you have to work as a team. It has to be a partnership in every sense of the word. This is especially true when both people in the relationship go out to work. It can't be that the wife comes home and does the cooking, cleaning, washing and ironing, and all the household tasks, to the point of exhaustion—it has to be a shared experience for it to work.

If you've never had to run a house before, it can be hard just simply working out the kind of everyday things that you need. You seem to end up with endless lists, and even stocking the cupboard with shopping can be a major task in itself, but when complete, it's truly satisfying.

The first time you invite family around for a meal can be a time of great tension and worry, but hopefully as time goes on, you'll realise that people have to accept you as they find you. If you relax, then so will your guests.

A thought:

It's all too easy to think that everything in one's home has to be "perfect". Who are we trying to impress? Orderliness and cleanliness are important, of course, but not to the point of obsession or making guests feel uncomfortable. What price do we pay for a clean home when we haven't got time to give attention to the things that matter, like that cuddle, curled up on the sofa, watching a favourite television programme? We lose something if we say, 'I haven't the time.'

A prayer:

Lord, as the couple embark on their new life together, may they delight in each other, may they freely share with each other all that they have, and all that they are willing to give. May it be a time of mutual respect, the giving and receiving, one to the other. Let their home be a place of welcome, where their love can be freely shared. Let it be a place where You also dwell, so that what is done in their home is done for the love of You and the love of others.

The Not So Festive Season

When the "in-laws" decide to spend Christmas with you, it may be a time when you wish that you could escape, or it may be a time of rejoicing, but one thing is for certain—it'll be a time of tension, if only because there's a desire to make it all "come right". If it happens to be your first Christmas as a couple then all I can say is… May God help you! I hope His presence will be truly there at your side.

The next question is, which of the in-laws should you have to stay? Often, if you elect to go with one, then the others are offended. This is the time when you wish you could cut yourself up in little bits, but sadly the Good Lord has not given us that ability. Each of the families will come with their own Christmas traditions, whilst you'll be trying to do things your way. The various families are often not accepting of the change so, if you push the boat out you'll be told you're going over the top, and if you keep it simple, not spending too much, you may be told you're not very generous, or even mean. Either way—you can't win…so just be yourself.

My attitude has always been that if the food is good, the house is warm, and the company is fun, then what's there to complain about? It's a time when people become fraught, people shop for Christmas as though they are shopping for a siege, and the supermarket will never open its doors again. Well, stuff the turkey! What really matters is, whether you've got a fire extinguisher to put out the flaming pudding, and whether you might need to douse your visitors!

If we're not careful, we can forget what the Christmas season is really supposed to be about. I feel that Christmas, doesn't start until I hear the service of Nine Lessons and Carols from Kings College Chapel, Cambridge, on Christmas Eve, and then attending midnight service, so that we put Christmas within the family of the church. Of course, there will be many who don't put Christ at the centre of the festive season, and if that's how you choose to see Christmas, well, that's fine for you, but how do we, among all the trappings, keep focused on what Christmas should really be about, which is giving love and care to others, especially those in need of some help or other?

I can never appreciate Christmas unless I've done something to support work for homeless people. When we have so much, it's important to realise that there are those who have so little. Christmas is a time when cracks in family life appear, because groups are thrown together over several days, people often drink too much and get too rowdy—even a board game can cause its own particular tensions. Children can get fractious because they have so much that they don't know how to handle it. It's often easier to give them a couple of presents each day, rather than masses all at once, so they don't get too excited.

There's something wonderful about bringing in the Christmas tree and the decorations. It's magical to turn on the lights and brighten a dark corner. Is that what it's like when God is part of our lives? There is the lightened corner, which gives a different quality to the house. At Christmas time, when we have so much, we also have so much to thank God for—

the lovely presents, the food, and the companionship of people that we love and that we choose to share our lives with.

When Christmas is over, you will breathe a sigh of relief, because your home is back to normal and you can just be with each other. What a precious gift that is.

A thought:

When Christmas becomes a non-flexible friend, and your credit card is truly bent, and instead of Christmas bells all you can hear are cash registers ringing in your ears—stop! Pause, remember what it is really about—the fact that God sent his only son into the world as a living form so that we could identify with him, and receive the Messiah as a little child, humbly coming into the world in poor circumstances. Although Christ was given gold, frankincense and myrrh, all of them precious gifts, he wasn't on the treadmill of bigger and better presents for more and more cost.

A prayer:

Lord, for so many, Christmas starts around September, in terms of planning, and it becomes a mind-stretching experience, of what we can give our relatives or friends, that's either acceptable or unique. Lord, there will be many travelling hundreds of miles to be with relatives—there will be high expectations of a "Happy Christmas". For many, that expectation will fall sadly short, the "bonhomie" isn't there. Help us get Christmas in perspective, let it be a time when we can be with our families, or friends, delighting in their company. May the gifts that we give be joyfully accepted, and may people be grateful for them. May we never forget those who are less fortunate than ourselves, and do all we can, not just at Christmas time, but at other times of the year too, to help them.

Family Squabbles

It's been my experience that there are two main issues on family squabbles—one is money, and the other is sibling rivalry.

It seems to matter where you come in the family hierarchy, the one in the middle seems to have a better time of it all. Sibling rivalry is real, and not some figment of the imagination of psychologists, we're all jostling for position, each finding our own way. It's tough when one of the group wants to strike out and do the unexpected, finding their own feet and their own path. When one of the siblings doesn't conform to the norm, it can put the whole family out of kilter.

Parents are in a difficult position here. How do you give encouragement and support in equal measure to your loved ones? Surely it has to be judged at the time according to need, but if one of the siblings is seen to be favoured more than the other, then the quarrels can start. They not only start, but they seem to continue for years to come, and mistakes made are eternally remembered.

Add into the equation issues concerning money, and you have a recipe for disaster! The real question is, how do you keep harmony in a difficult situation? It all comes down to respect and love. If we respect our sibling's individuality and love them for it, having admiration when they are creatively different, then this relationship that could be perpetually in a state of disharmony will suddenly be truly melodic.

When a family works well together, pulls together and loves together, it really is like the completed jigsaw that creates a beautiful picture. It's sad when one piece is missing, when one member of the family is either excommunicated in reality, or feels that way. It's an area that has to be worked on, it doesn't just happen. The only way is to not let the pain and hurt that individuals can suffer to fester and grow, by talking about issues, the boil is lanced, and hopefully peace will reign.

Often, when you talk to people about their family, and the quarrels that have gone on over the years and you ask 'What caused the problem?' they will often say that they can't remember what started it—they can only remember the consequence. It's usually kept bubbling because one individual is trying to take control and may, in some cases, are so buoyed by their own power because of their own inadequacy.

A thought:

In the end, it all comes down to communication. A recognition that people's feelings matter, however trivial the issue may seem to somebody else. We should never disregard someone's hurt feelings, we should acknowledge them and try to ease the pain.

A prayer:

Lord, when the family is seen as a warring faction, give one person the strength, and the patience, to try and intercede on any or all of the others' behalf. Let all voices be heard, all views felt and understood, even if to some they may seem irrelevant. Don't let materialism get in the way of the issues that really matter. Please, Lord, let the family quarrel be resolved before a serious crisis comes, so that all thoughts of what caused the row in the first place get forgotten.

Help them all to have a determination to get to the bottom of the problem, so that harmony can be restored, and those who have been hurt, refreshed and renewed.

Is Money the Root of All Evil?

One of the biggest contentions in family life seems to be the subject of money. You either have it or you don't—those who have it are resented by those who don't. The next question is, what to do if you do have it? Do I support my family whilst I can see what they're doing with it—or wait until I'm gone?

If wills are not prepared then it's pretty certain it'll be a battle between family members! The answer is that there are no pockets in a shroud, you can't take it with you, and there's no point in being the richest person in the cemetery. Sure, we'll need money for a rainy day, and funds to deal with our old age, particularly now that social care needs are being cut back, but I can think of nothing finer than to help your family or anyone else along life's way. That doesn't mean that you "spoon feed", it means that you give them a helping hand when times are hard, it may be your way of appreciating the help that you've been given, for one reason or another over time.

For a parent to constantly say, 'I don't have any money' when you know that they do is extremely hard and very difficult to live with, it does nothing for relationships. To see a parent act like George Elliot's Silas Marner is extremely frustrating. There's a moral in this story. Silas learnt, to his cost, that the daily counting of his money did nothing for him. Eventually, someone came along and stole it, but when he found the love of another human being, in this case a tiny child whom he cared for, he realised that money wasn't important. Money is only as good as what you can do with it. John Wesley, in his sermon on money, said 'Earn all you can, save all you can, give all you can.' There is nothing more joyous than to see what financial help, given in the right way, can do to support another human being.

It isn't about how much money one parent can give to a family member, it's all about the love, care and time that the parent, or family member, gives to the person in need. There will be those, of course, who want what they think is rightfully theirs handed to them on a plate. Maybe they're not prepared to work for what they need, because it can come easy from Mum or Dad. This is wrong. We need to value not only the money but value ourselves. If it comes easy we don't appreciate it, if we have to save up and work for something then we buy it with pride.

A thought:

I can remember the very first piece of jewellery that I purchased. I used to go into the shop and pay off five pounds here, ten pounds there—it took me over six months to buy a beautiful brooch. I was overjoyed when I took it from the shop. I still have it to this day, and love it, not just for the beauty of the piece, but for what it represented—hard-fought and hard-won. In my case, there was a certain level of pride that it came, not from a free handout, but out of my salary, which I had carefully put to one side to purchase this pretty object. We appreciate items much more when we taste the personal victory of working for them.

A prayer:

Lord, there's much disharmony and bickering in families over money. One person is angry because another family member has more than they do, but at the end of the day, it's so pointless. Parents need to be aware how their actions can affect their children and cause hurt. Help parents to be more mindful of the needs of their children, and help children not to assume that what their parents have worked for, should automatically be theirs. The life that You gave us is for living and for enjoyment, help us not to waste the time that You have given us through pointless bickering. Lord, help us not to be obsessed by what everything costs, for when we do, we lose the beautiful sentiment behind it.

The Gift

Several years into the marriage, there will be words said by eager prospective grandparents, friends or relations, as to why the couple don't have the patter of tiny feet around the home. This, of course, may be their choice. They may just want to be together and only have eyes for one another, and live their life with the sole purpose of pleasing each other. There is absolutely nothing wrong in this, if this is what they choose.

However, certain people think it's acceptable to make jokes or comments that are not helpful. In certain cases the couple may deeply desire a child but, for whatever reason, it doesn't happen. It doesn't matter what the cause is, or who needs help—what matters, is that the couple are free to work through this difficulty in their own way, and in their own time.

There will be those who will say, 'Well, it's fun trying,' but the pressure of trying and failing is enormous. If the couple decide to go down the route of fertility treatment, it will be a long, hard road, with much embarrassment, pain and worry about the outcome. It's a roller-coaster ride in every sense of the word, a roller-coaster ride of mood swings, caused by surges of hormones, along with bouts of depression.

The couple have to be very supportive of each other. Sometimes couples don't stay the course, their difficult journey can be helped so much by the people who take their hand along the way. All too often, friends and family are too ready to give their opinion, and to smooth it all over by saying, if it hasn't worked, 'Never mind, you can try again.' It takes guts, determination, courage, and very often money, to pick yourself up from the floor, and have another go. I'm sure that there are many couples who, after the first attempt, say it isn't worth the emotional stress.

Children aren't ours by "right"—they are a gift sent from God. We are custodians of their little lives to help them along the way, to protect and nurture them and, more importantly, to love them. However, if we're not given this most precious gift, then we may have to make an incredibly difficult choice. Perhaps we have the ability to be wonderful foster-parents or adoptive parents, giving love and family life to a child in need, a child who has been disadvantaged for all kinds of reasons.

We have to be sensitive to those people who, when they see a small child, long for it to be theirs, to hold it and nurture it, and understand their emotional grief when it can't be theirs. This predicament is almost like bereavement. So many people have an opinion, so many people will make platitudes and meaningless statements—meaningless because they have never experienced it themselves, or even known someone who walked that path.

One thing we must never do is make the couple feel inadequate. We must love them through it and be a listening ear, and, of course, we must rejoice with them when it all comes right, thanks to modern scientific advances.

A thought:

I'm conscious that I have to be mindful of the words I put on the paper. This is also important for those who know someone who may be struggling with this issue. It's all too easy to go in where angels fear to tread, usually feet first, saying and doing the wrong thing. Allow the couple to work it through themselves, give them the space and time, and loving environment, by which they can approach you with their problem. Give them all the help they need, especially financial. Fertility treatment can be extremely costly, if only with fares and transport, going backwards and forwards for clinical appointments. Don't condemn them or, more importantly, don't compare them with other members of your family; that will only serve to make them feel inadequate.

A prayer:

Lord, we know that the gift of a child, and the gift of life, is a gift from You, which is something so wonderful, precious, and unique. Lord, thanks to modern science, those childless couples might have the opportunity of being blessed with such a glorious little bundle of joy. To all those who are embarking on this difficult treatment, may You give them "stickability".

May You give them the strength and courage to go forward and seek help, give them a sense of togetherness, one supporting the other in times of trial. If treatment isn't successful, give them the courage to try again, or if they decide not to pursue continuing bouts of fertility treatment, give them the serenity of spirit, and peace of mind, to accept their fate and move on, knowing that You'll love them with or without a child.

Pregnancy

When the wife suspects that she may be pregnant and gets the first positive test before going to the doctor, this can be a time of great joy or trepidation. As a counsellor, if I had someone tell me they were pregnant, I made sure I didn't fall into the trap of believing that she was overjoyed. The classic counselling question 'How do you feel about that' is, of course, one way to give someone permission to express that they're not happy at all.

Let's assume that when it is confirmed the couple are ecstatic, overjoyed, hugging each other with delight. Usually they want to keep it to themselves for a few weeks, just in case something goes wrong. This is a very special moment in their life together, a time when the marriage has three in it, or should I say four? And it's a time when we should thank God for the precious moment and the precious gift.

When the couple "spills the beans", other members of the family show how thrilled they are, usually grandparents want to go around buying so many things for the new arrival, and, of course, choosing the right wallpaper and decor for the nursery is incredibly important. This is where family members usually come into their own—helping to decorate, this "buzz" of activity seems to be part of the rite of passage, the joy of preparation. However, there's the worry, the responsibility, praying that mother and baby will be well, and everything will go according to plan. There's that incredible moment when you see this tiny being on the scan, and realise God's perfect creation, it can also be a moment when you anxiously wait to know that all is well with the little one.

Mothers craving for the most unusual food combinations, or other things, usually cause much laughter. A great deal of how the mother will deal with her pregnancy depends upon her attitude to it, if she believes that God has made pregnancy the most natural act in the world, then God willing, she will sail through it.

There is obviously much apprehension, tension and worry coming up to the time of the birth—especially if you're the father! The bag is packed and unpacked several times, people are put on red alert for that night-time call—why so many are born in the early hours of the morning I'm yet to understand! Naturally there are many difficult processes to go through before baby is here, yet, although the pain of birth is often traumatic, it's one that is soon forgotten when the baby is placed into the mother's arms. The sense of wonderment that mother and father feel as they gaze lovingly at their little one is a perfect moment.

What joy!—A complete little family, a new beginning and an opportunity where the child can bring much happiness to parents, grandparents, and friends alike.

A thought:

There's a tendency for grandparents to want to take over, they feel that they are helping, and that they have years of knowledge to impart. This, of course, is absolutely true, but new parents have to find their own way. It's great that fathers also have paternity leave now, so that they can bond with their child right from the start and give their wife a helping hand when she's most in need of a rest. The bond we make with our children at this time is a bond that should last throughout the child's life. Everything is new, challenging, exciting and frightening, all at the same time. The responsibility seems awesome, but we have a unique opportunity to enhance a tiny person's life, and what a privilege that is.

A prayer:

Lord, when we look at that tiny child and we touch those perfectly formed fingers and toes, we can't fail but be amazed. Tiny fingernails that are fascinating to see and that gorgeous new baby smell, as we hold this wonderful being, we realise how vulnerable and precious they are. We thank you Lord for your creation, and for the many blessings that this child will bring to its parents and family alike.

Lord, bless the child. Give fortitude to the parents as they cope with sleepless nights, and have to deal with the overwhelming tiredness. Give them gentleness, patience and love for this tiny child who did not ask to come into the world. It's their responsibility to do all they can to help them to go down the right path in your name.

Family Christening

When a new member of the family arrives, it's a very exciting time. Even more exciting is the rite of passage in terms of the child's progression through life. Some people may make the decision to have their child blessed, leaving them to make up their own minds as to the Christian faith in later life. Others will feel that to have their child baptized is a necessary part of Christian life, to give their child a sense of a new life in Christ. The symbolism of water, which is the act of cleansing from the old world into the new, is a very important one, and just as important, are the promises made by parents and godparents, or sponsors as they are now called, and the congregation, on behalf of the child.

The words of the baptismal service are very thought-provoking because in today's world, we need more Christian values and the sense in which we're helping to keep this child on the right path. It's therefore important that those who make the vows on behalf of the child, do so earnestly.

Another good aspect of a christening is that there'll be many people, who wouldn't normally move in church circles, but they are there to support the family and share in the celebration, therefore the preacher has a unique opportunity to make his words count, and give a clear Christian message to those who wouldn't normally hear it. If we only change the mind of one person that day, then the service has done its work, and the little one has started on the right path of

Christian teaching throughout his or her life. One element of the christening is the celebration that follows, its right and fitting that family and friends bless this child.

A thought:

The christening isn't about naming the child, naming the child in public is only for the benefit of the congregation. It's the opportunity for the family members to stand up and be counted as Christians in a world where Christian values are becoming less and less evident, and less and less meaningful. If we really take on board Christian teaching in the baptismal service we'll have a charter for life that can see us through many trials and tribulations. No one knows what the future holds for this little one, we only know that with the blessing of Christ behind them they have the values that will stand the test of time.

A prayer:

Lord, when we think of a child coming for baptism, they haven't been spoilt by the nasty things that can occur in our world, and they have no means of knowing, at this early stage in their life, Christian values. We, as members of the congregation, are custodians of Christ's teaching, so, help us to really care for this child. Help us meet its needs when its parents or grandparents can no longer meet them, and help us support the child through its life and be true to the congregational responses that we make on the child's behalf on this very special day in their life.

Grandparents

To suddenly find that you're a grandparent for the first time is a very happy state to be in. I don't know why we always congratulate the grandparents on how clever they have been, when the outcome had nothing to do with them, other than the fact that they gave birth to one of the parents! But nevertheless, this tiny new member of the family is something that they can boast about, and bring out all manner of photographs, occasionally boring the pants off all their friends.

It's as though they and the baby are the only child and grandparents in the world. What's wrong with that? Nothing at all provided it's in proportion. This is the time when they can spend more time with the grandchildren than they did with their own children—this is the time for fun without discipline, a time when the grandchild can wind grandma and grandad around their little finger.

It's a time when grandparents can see when Mum and Dad need a break, it's a time when they can look after the grandchild and give the parents back their own individual identity, if only for a night, a time for spoiling, a time for loving. This is the opportunity to give the child all the time it needs to learn and delight in it.

To be a grandparent means that you can spend more time with the child, delighting in its development and rejoicing in the child's newfound discovery—a favourite toy, the love of insects and adventures in the garden, usually the things that make the child mucky! It's the special things that grandparents and grandchildren do together—the chats in the car, and those inevitable answers to the question 'Why?'

The great joy for a grandparent is to help their loved one discover the world around them, the trips up to London to see the sights, maybe their first experience of going to a pantomime or a play—all the things that Mum and Dad might not have time for in a busy life. It's also the time for giving a child a way back to Mum or Dad, who have been cross with them, and the grandchild might feel fearful of knowing how to approach their parent. Grandparents can be wonderful mediators in this regard, putting an old head on young shoulders, and teaching them all manner of skills.

They are also the people, very often, who give the special treats. Mum and Dad may be very particular about too much cake, fizzy drinks and sweets, but grandparents often are the ones who give in. It's great when they are generous to the grandchildren, but they too must remember that they are not there to take the place of the parent; rather, they are there as an enhancement of parenthood, a kind of custodian when Mum and Dad can't be around for whatever reason.

Their role is not to take over, but to fill in, they are there also as an assurance factor, when Mum and Dad feel unsure and insecure, and they are also there in times of crisis, illness, to be a steadying and guiding hand. Most of all, grandparents should aim to be a friend to all concerned—parents and children alike, they are also there to be proud and give encouragement and love.

The tuck-in at night and the bedtime story are extra special when given by Nanny and Granddad, and they are there as the child's rock and strength and, I pray, teaching them good Christian values that will last them through to later life.

A thought:

Thank God for grandparents! Let us never see them as objects of interference, but as support and strength, wisdom and encouragement. It's important that they too have their day in the celebration of this tiny child, they need something to be proud of, but, more importantly, they need a sense of fulfilment and purpose. This tiny child gives a whole new meaning to life because we now have a life with purpose in it, the purpose is to see your grandchild grow into adulthood and then have children of their own, what a privilege.

A prayer:

Lord, we thank you for our grandparents, who will be there for our children, hopefully loving them and nurturing them all the way through into adulthood. As much as we love them, Lord, we ask that they will be ever mindful of the fact that they are not the parents of our children; we pray, Lord, that they will always be there for us to approach, to ask advice, and that they will freely offer their help. But Lord, we must also help them to understand lovingly that whilst we appreciate the help, we sometimes want to be free to make our own decisions about our child, even if they disapprove.

Lord, when this relationship becomes difficult, help us be diplomatic and understanding, not squashing their enthusiasm, but hoping that they will see that this relationship is a partnership. Bless them, Lord, for who they are and help them know that even if there is conflict, there is still so much love.

Child's Early Years

There's nothing more wonderful than to watch your child grow, and respond to both of you as parents, and the world around them. The wonderful laughter when a small child finds something amusing and really chuckles makes you feel glad to be alive, and glad that you are sharing in the child's discovery of the world and people around them.

Each newly discovered task that is accomplished is greeted with joy. Each new taste of something that the child puts into its mouth and either spits out in disgust, or relishes its texture and flavour, is a delight. Not so delightful, is when he or she decides to throw the contents of their dish onto the floor in a paddy! But it's all part of the growing process. What a wonderful privilege to be able to help a child develop into a social being. Those first tentative steps that are very wobbly are incredible to watch—nature is marvellous in the way it knows when it's time for the child to let go, and stand on their own two feet, both physically and metaphorically.

Language is so complicated, yet it's a voyage of discovery. How amusing it seems when the child is struggling to formulate words and sentences, and gets them round the wrong way, and, of course, we have the inevitable 'Why?' questions. Everything is 'Why?' Almost to the point of distraction for the parents. Yet it's the time when you can really see the child's brain working to assimilate information and grasp understanding. It's a time when we, as adults, can influence and educate in a good way—what a privilege.

As the child develops, it becomes less dependent, less clingy, and wants to explore. It's fantastic when they make their first friends, other than brothers and sisters, such a special skill that will stand them in good stead in later life. Everything is a time of exploration, when they are tiny, most things go into the mouth, and this can be frightening for onlookers, but they soon learn what tastes right.

Visiting nursery school for the first time is a whole new world, frightening for the child, and a rite of passage for the parents. The separation anxiety on both sides is enormous, the child wanting reassurance by first rushing to find out what is there, and then running back to Mummy or Daddy, rather like having a foot in both camps. How lovely it is to experience paint, sand and play dough, and all those messy toys. It doesn't matter that they go home mucky, they've had great fun.

Nursery school is obviously the precursor to stepping out into the wider world. That first morning when the child is left at "big school", and feels desolate, and you can't hide your tears, but have to walk away, is a defining moment in the child's life, and is the first stepping stone to adulthood.

It's an amazing moment when your child brings home the first picture or card made for you, so precious that it's treasured and kept for many years. The first gift that you receive in this way that your child makes with so much love is really special, it doesn't matter how amateurish it may seem, because it's given with love.

A thought:

In this time, when we have to be mindful of children's safety at all times and in all situations, the innocent picture that I've created here may seem too idyllic. Yet it's important to remember that for the vast majority of children, this will be what their early years will be like. It's important that we still know how to comfort and nurture, and not be afraid to give that child the loving security that it needs.

I realise that some people may read this not having experienced a loving childhood, and it may be difficult for them to see this picture. However, when it's their turn to give loving responses to their own children, they have the chance to redress the balance in a most magnificent way.

A prayer:

Lord, the gift of a child is such a precious thing, but we're only guardians looking after them until they can take care of themselves. Help us to make the right decisions, in the best interest of the child, and not in the best interest of ourselves. Help us to have a balanced viewpoint, loving patience, kindness, and gentleness—all the qualities that you advocated in the gifts of the spirit.

If we really tried to live by that standard, then we will do right by our child, or those children that we care for. Help us always to be there for them, support and encourage them in every way, so that they may grow into worthwhile, responsible human beings, with a zest for life, and an appreciation of Your wonderful world.

When Your Child Goes
Into Hospital

It's hard enough for any of us to have to go into hospital and face surgery, but when it's a tiny child it seems so traumatic, particularly when you can't make them understand what's happening. The environment can often seem very threatening, noisy and strange with people that they don't know handling them, and not always being gentle. Medical procedures are invasive and alien to everything that they know, and are not only difficult for the child, but can be distressing for the parents—and the clinicians. No one wants to see their child struggling for whatever reason, and it's a time when we feel helpless, because we have to put our child into the care of someone who has more knowledge about their situation than we do.

It's a time of upheaval and worry, but it's a time when we have to trust that due to the medical knowledge of the doctors, our child will be well. Hospital staff are usually extremely caring on a children's ward, and they do all they can to support parents, and those who have a close connection with the sick child.

In fact, the modern day practice is to assign a key worker, or child nurse, to one particular set of parents, and stay with them until their child's difficulties have been resolved. We feel helpless when someone we love is wheeled down a corridor to the operating theatre, but we have to put our faith in the surgeons and clinicians caring for our child, that all will be well. We are never more relieved than when the child comes round from the anaesthetic, and wants their parents to be there.

Recovery may be difficult, and sometimes painful. It's hard to explain to a little one what's going on, yet, we have to support them, be there for them and love them through it, even when times are hard. Through the modern techniques of surgery, healing can be truly miraculous, something in which we can marvel at man's cleverness, but we also have to own that when times are tough, this relationship has four in it, parents, child and God, and we must never forget those additional friends and loved ones, who give support as they anxiously wait outside in the corridor or back at home.

When the child comes home from hospital, there will be a level of anxiety. Hospitals give everyone concerned a sense of security—one push of the alarm button means that help is at hand. Back at home it can feel a scary place when that prop has been taken away, but it's the place where loving and nurturing can continue to take place—the little treats that make the child feel important and special, because they've been ill, and the kindly things that parents, grandparents and friends do to ease the passage back to health.

A thought:

Paediatric medical care is truly amazing because so often the child can't tell you what's wrong, and parents are often too distraught to fully articulate the issues. Those who have a special feeling for this work are to be highly praised. Hospitals such as Great Ormond Street Hospital for Sick

Children, have pioneered the way in medical techniques for children—for that we should always be thankful.

A prayer:

Lord, when a child goes into hospital, let it be a place of kindness and gentleness. May they quickly find that they are able to forget the discomfort, and feel better. May they make new friends in the hospital ward. For the parents, give them courage and strength to cope with the difficult days ahead. May they be close to one another, as they cope with the ordeal of dealing with the sick child, and may they rejoice at bringing that child home, restored to health.

Special Educational Needs

Every parent wants their child to do well at school, to succeed in examinations, and to make something of their future life. To some children, academia is a no-go area. Try as they might, they don't succeed, often their frustration transfers itself into anger and sometimes bullying, or an attitude of non-cooperation with their teachers.

I can remember from my own school days, when I was partially sighted, that coping with maths and reading small text was a nightmare. Appreciating the printed word through writing poetry and reading the words of beautiful hymns, kept me sane.

If your child freezes at the prospect of standing up in front of the class, reading some text, or struggling with spelling, and not making any real headway with reading, then perhaps the time has come to look a little further into the reasons as to why this is happening. It's not just because he or she is disruptive, there's a reason for their behaviour.

Your child's failure to cope with reading and writing may be for a number of reasons, all too often the child is labelled as dyslexic when there could be a multitude of medical, psychological or emotional issues. The key is to get an educational assessment done in order to have your child statemented as quickly as possible, so that he or she can receive the appropriate help.

No one knows your child better than you do, and they can also have great insight as to their difficulties. You want the best for your child and you may have a fight on your hands to get it, but don't be put off, help is out there, so be determined.

If your child has been diagnosed with dyslexia, there are some amazing computer programmes that "think" dyslexia, and help with dyslexic spelling, putting it right. I have had the privilege of knowing several seriously dyslexic people, who are highly intelligent, but when it comes to recognising the construction of words, they are just not there. Yet, with such help that is now available from the school, and other sources, a person with dyslexia can lead a near normal life.

Dyslexia does not mean that your child is not mentally capable. First and foremost, it is no one's fault, and by and large it can be overcome with skilful teaching and modern technology. The issue of seeking professional help within the educational system applies whatever the disability or issues that your child might have. Children with more physical disability often have complex needs, yet the issues are just the same in helping your child to become a more rounded and fully functioning person. Don't give up, put your trust in God and keep fighting, for your child is well worth fighting for.

A thought:

In this world of high academic achievement, we should spare a thought for those struggling to keep up, realising that the difficulty isn't a social stigma, but a medical problem.

A prayer:

Lord, give parents of children with special needs within education, the grace and determination to seek help, emotionally, medically and from the educational specialists. May the parents have the courage to seek advice, the will to keep on going, and be grateful for all the opportunities that are available.

Death of a Family Pet

The introduction of a pet into the family home is a highly significant moment; it can often be the time when the whole family feel a much closer bond because of a beloved dog or cat. Obviously, there are many more pets that become part of the family existence—even rats, snakes, and spiders, and many more obscure animals can be part of the so-called pet scene. When the animal becomes so much of a child's life, and then dies, it's often the first time that the child will be confronted with the issue of death and dying, and it's a painfully hard lesson to learn.

The child or children need to be able to say their goodbyes, and they need the ritual of laying the creature to rest in whatever way feels comfortable to them. I know that my step-grandchildren have a garden that has a particular pet's corner, with little crosses that mark the spot, with their pet's name. This is important because it gives closure, and it's often a rehearsal for dealing with greater bereavements in later life. Thinking of that, who am I to say that the loss of a pet goldfish is any less important than that of a person to a child? Actually, in their mind there's often no distinction, the two are equally important. When I lost my English cocker spaniel, Harvey, I was devastated.

I can remember an incident of a young man whose father died of cancer. At the time he showed little signs of grief, and coped very well—actually, he coped too well. Several months later, he went on holiday and came back to find that there had been a major power failure on his tropical fish tank, and all the fish had sadly died. He went into paroxysms of grief, sobbing to the very depth of his being—he was in a terrible state. Later, he admitted that this incident was the last straw. He couldn't cope with the death of his father, and had stuffed his feelings away, but when he saw the fish, it all came tumbling out, and he couldn't cope any more.

There's one important lesson here—that grief cannot be suppressed, at least not for too long. It has to come out, it has to be dealt with, and have an expression of closure. It's perfectly okay to grieve over what might seem trivial, we are where we are, and have to deal with grief on whatever level and at no specific time and we all need permission to grieve.

A thought:

Pets can transform our life; they give us the means of showing our affection, of expressing love and tenderness, and the opportunity to nurture something precious. Pets give us the opportunity to show gentleness and kindness, without feeling silly or stupid. We can tell them many things, share any thoughts and problems, in a way that we would perhaps not choose to share with another human being. Our secret is safe with them, it's not going to be embellished in conversation, or passed round to the masses. Pets give us unconditional love, which is very rare in our human life, but it's extremely precious.

A prayer:

Lord, we thank you for the gift of a beautiful pet, the dog or the cat that we can come home to, make a fuss of, and get a response from. They give us probably more pleasure than we give to them, they are incredibly special, and help to shape our life in so many ways. Having to walk the dog helps to keep us healthy, and give us an appreciation of Your world, a world that You created for all creatures, great and small, to live in.

Lord, help us to value the sanctity of life, in whatever form it takes. Lord, there are many creatures, millions in fact, that have still not been discovered, yet alone named, but when we come across them, help us to value them and appreciate them for what they can do in our world.

When we sadly have to say goodbye to a beloved pet, help us remember, with gratitude, the love that we shared together.

Teenage Years

It's hard for an adult to remember what it was like to be a teenager. I think one of the most agonising aspects is when the rest of the family use you as a butt for their teasing and jokes. It's a time when the young teenager is often painfully shy, and blushes at the least provocation; it's also the time when they pass between childhood and adulthood extremely quickly.

For the boys, it's much worse when the voice starts to break—one minute it's high pitched and squeaky, the next minute, bass, and very masculine-sounding and "down in the boots"! At this time they often don't know where they are. Their body image now assumes great importance with up-to-the-minute clothing and the latest aftershave, of course. When they experience shaving for the first time, they're often the butt of Dad's jokes, but it's also a time when they find their feet, work out their own identity, and experiment with each other. For some, this may not be as easy as it would first appear, yet they would never admit it to their peer group. It takes courage to be different; it's easy to go along with the crowd.

I can remember that I took a great deal of stick from my family and others because I wanted to listen to classical music when everyone else was listening to the Beatles and the Rolling Stones. My age has been given away by that previous sentence, but nevertheless, I can remember how painful it was to go through those life-changing experiences, your whole world is turned upside down and you're constantly questioning how others see you.

Later in life, you won't really care, but at this point everything matters, it's the time when you'll really show the person you are, and your overall development. Naturally, if it's your teenage daughter going through this, you'll want to protect her, making sure she doesn't get taken advantage of or get in with the wrong crowd. But there's a sense in which we have to allow our teenage children to grow, and we have to genuinely remember what it was like in our day.

Times have changed, sadly not always for the better. Our values have also changed, but we're now in a fast-moving world with high expectations. Children as young as fourteen can often look much older; they dress in a very mature way and they know exactly how they want to look. Fashion magazines have not always helped the situation by presenting a body image of people who are airbrushed to unrealistic perfection. Now, hopefully, there's a little more realism here, and the message is just be yourself, be the person you are or the person you want to be, and don't worry about conforming to the norm. See your body as a precious gift, treat it with respect in all senses and live a healthy lifestyle.

A thought:

Young teenagers will find this passage of time in their life incredibly hard, yet it's also a time for excitement, a time to discover oneself, a time to be carefree and happy, but a time to think of the wider world and those within it. Teenage years can be selfish years if we let them be, but they can also be incredibly productive and give you a sense of belonging and purpose.

A prayer:

Lord, I have tried to think of the many positive things to do with being a teenager, but I'm also aware of those young people who are struggling. They struggle because in finding their own identity, it often creates tension with parents and pressures at home for one reason or another. Help these young people to realise that they are part of the family unit, and not separated from it. Help them to find their own independence and identity, yet be respectful of parents and people older than themselves. Help them not to be crippled by their embarrassment, but help them to strike out for what they believe in, and be principled. Let them be people that their families can be proud of, and give them a smooth passage into adulthood.

God and Our Dirty Socks

When I was a child, my two brothers shared a large bedroom in our three-bedroom house in the East End of London. It was easy to tell whose bed was whose; one side of the room was always neat and tidy, like a new pin—everything put away and everything in its place. On the other side of the room, it looked like a war zone—total chaos, clothing dropped on the floor, shoes strewn all over the place, with no sense of order whatsoever. Mum would despair, constantly moaning about putting dirty socks and washing in the laundry basket and keeping the room tidy.

Dad would help Mum at weekends with the vacuuming and polishing, but when he reached the boys' bedroom, you would hear the voices go up. I vividly recall that one day, Dad became so angry that he threw the shoes down the stairs, opened the street door and threw the pairs of shoes into the street with my brother at his heels, frantically trying to retrieve them! This seemed a little drastic—after all, one doesn't want to air one's dirty linen in public.

It's something that has been indelibly etched in all our minds, and it's something that I wouldn't wish to repeat. However, it does call into question the responsibility that we also have to those who look after us in teenage life. Why should our parents be our slaves? They will have a far easier existence if we play our part in family life and cooperate with the rules of the house. I think it's necessary to have ground rules, it gives a sense of boundary but, more importantly, it gives a sense of respect. Respecting those who are older than ourselves and the environment in which we live is a pre-requisite for later life, therefore it's extremely important.

It's not just about dirty socks or shoes strewn across a room, it's about our own self-esteem and how we wish to present ourselves to others in the world. After all, if our bedroom is normally a tip, what does that say for how we will behave in a holiday situation when we have to share our room with somebody else? Not all of us will have the luxury of private, single room accommodation. There's quite a lesson here about how we co-exist with each other, chaos can bring happiness but, more often than not, it brings discontentment and anger from others.

When we are in the midst of our own chaos, we don't see it. We have to be mindful of what it does to other people and try to make them feel comfortable with the situation. Perhaps the respect that we feel for our elders only truly comes when we are approaching a similar landmark—what the answer is I'm not certain, yet one thing I know for sure is that if all concerned are made to feel valued and loved, and part of the family network, then that chaos will be part of a fun-loving house and not one of discord.

A thought:

Sometimes parents have to make snap, yet difficult decisions, regarding the lessons that they teach to their children. They are often hard-fought and hard-won, with the battle lines not clearly drawn. Sometimes all it takes is a moment of empathy, a moment of reconciliation for difficult situations to get resolved and for those concerned to have a greater understanding between them. Life isn't just about creating difficult atmospheres, it's about a happy environment and happiness around those that you love. So, when you feel like storming out in protest and you haven't the time to do the daily chores or, more importantly, to listen, think again.

A prayer:

Lord, it's so vital that the messages that we give to our children are good ones, ones that will help them through the rest of their life. Give us the wisdom, the strength, and the courage to know when it's right to explode and when it's right to keep our counsel. When the situation is chaotic, help us to put both sides of the coin, and teach our children to appreciate the things that they do have, rather than moan about things that they don't have. Help us to love through the chaos, even when it's difficult and realise that our children enrich our lives beyond measure. Help us to truly appreciate them, and value them, for their uniqueness.

Watching for Dangers

Those teenage years, and beyond, are probably some of the most worrying for parents. They always fall between two schools, on the one hand protecting and nurturing, and on the other, giving their child space and freedom to develop and be their own unique self. There are so many pressures on youngsters to conform and go along with the crowd.

When you're young, you don't want to stand out as unique or as an individual, you want to merge and certainly wouldn't want to be seen as being a killjoy. So when groups are gathered together in clubs, or on street corners, or of course, the inevitable pub, it's hard to say to a member of your peer group that you don't want yet another drink, even more importantly, that you don't want to be legless.

I have to be honest and say that I've never seen the point of drinking oneself into oblivion, because there are issues, or situations, that one would rather forget, so it's better to stay alert and face the issues head on. Heavy drinking, with its inherent health problems, is bad enough, but combined with drugs, and all the issues that that can bring, parents have a terribly worrying time.

I can't imagine what it must feel like when, as a parent, you notice the tell-tale signs of drug use, and then start to go searching for the evidence. When your child becomes dependent upon the drugs and needs money for a daily fix, it must be unimaginable hell.

Sadly, it happens all too often and there isn't enough support for parents and families. Detoxing programmes are available, but there is often a long waiting list, and the person needs to prove their commitment to break free of the habit, before they are accepted onto the programme for detoxification, so, it's a long, hard road for parents and young people alike.

Often, because of drugs, there's a huge personality change. There are also problems with weight, and loss of appetite—these symptoms are terribly worrying to parents, who want to see their children healthy. At this point, parents are often rejected by their children, yet, it's the time when they are needed most, it's the time when they should stand together in adversity.

It's very difficult for people to come to terms with this situation. Because this illness or adversity is self-inflicted, those of us who don't have to cope with it may not be so sympathetic. The human body, when it's working well, is a very finely balanced machine, it doesn't want or need highly toxic chemicals poured into it unnecessarily, it's all about young people valuing and appreciating what they have, and not abusing it.

So many of the types of problems that I've spoken about come out of an identity crisis, lack of confidence, a sense of not wanting to be the person they are, wanting to be someone entirely different. They think that the "quick-fix" of drugs or alcohol will solve their problems. Of course, it won't, it'll only make matters far worse.

When a person is in this predicament, they don't need rejection by family, they need encouragement, and to be embraced by those who love them. Sometimes, we may never know the cause of such trauma. The waste of a life, and the financial burden, although I suspect there will be those who will say that to take drugs, or drink to excess, isn't a waste of life. What is a waste is not appreciating what we've been given, in terms of a fit and healthy body, so that we can use it to its fullest advantage.

A thought:

Many of us will have seen the consequences of drugs and alcohol abuse on our streets and within the family, and will have seen the results of it through domestic violence. People, when they reach rock bottom, may end up on the street, then all too often we see the consequences of living such a life. There are many organisations helping people who have come to this point in their life. The Salvation Army and St Martin's in the Fields in London are doing sterling work in this regard.

As the lucky ones, we should do whatever we can to support this kind of work. It really is a case of being a Good Samaritan, and not walking by on the other side of the road, but stopping to help, giving friendship, and binding the wounds, whether they be on a physical, or emotional, level. When we know of someone in trouble, we should do all we can to support them and we should also befriend their family, for they are bereft, lonely, confused and concerned. Especially when it happens to a family who seemingly have had many opportunities, yet the person who has become addicted has rejected those opportunities. We may never know the reason why it occurred, it doesn't really matter; what matters is what we do now to bring that person back into the fold.

A prayer:

Lord, for all those people suffering from any kind of addiction that has brought them to their knees, on a physical or emotional level, help them to realise that the only way now is up. The only way forward is to change and seek a new way of working, and a new way of living. Lord, help them to realise that they have a right to take their place in the world, help them to realise that they matter to You, every last one of them. Give them the courage to seek refuge and help, and give them the resolve to keep working at it, even if they have false starts. This is their first step on the road to recovery.

Lord, give them the friends along the way, that they will desperately need, if they are to lick this problem and stand on their own two feet. And Lord, I thank You for all those people working in addiction clinics, up and down the land, working with the homeless on the streets of our major cities, befriending them, and looking after their medical needs. May they find You, not necessarily in the Christian word, but in the Christian deed, one person to another, giving genuine outreach to those who may have got so low that they aren't in a position to ask for help themselves.

Give those support workers the courage to keep going when it all seems pointless, and may they never stop working until addiction is no more. I know, Lord, that this would be utopia, but nevertheless, we can strive for it in our desire to want a world of happy people around us.

Social Isolation

Not long ago when you travelled in your car, you found a public telephone box to let people know that you had reached your destination. When you went on holiday, you sent a postcard to let people know that you had arrived safely, and wishing they were there, although not really! Just thirty years on, the communication network has changed beyond all recognition, change that I couldn't have imagined as a child. Now we can't go anywhere without our mobile phone constantly ringing in our ears, or having the use of our all-singing, all-dancing mobile devices, keeping us constantly in touch with emails and other aspects of communication or business.

There's a sense in which I feel like saying "ouch!" No wonder our brains need to rest, it's a case of stop the world I want to get off. Perhaps this is why retreats are becoming more popular, people long for that sense of tranquillity. The internet is a fantastic tool for finding out information, and keeping people in touch, but there's almost too much information, and young people in particular are spending many hours in front of a computer screen. This can be incredibly worrying for parents. What are they looking at when they trawl through the internet; are all the websites savoury and helpful?

We've heard of some horrendous acts perpetrated on the internet, often involving young people. Another source of alarm for parents. It's important that they keep watch on what their children are searching for, more importantly, it's vital that they help their child to strike a balance between technical communication, and the interaction of a human kind. Many young people are losing personal confidence, they rely on the safety of the keyboard, and not on the social skills that have to be learnt if they are to do well in the workplace, and in business.

However much we might say that the internet is the way to go, there's still no substitute for that one-to-one meeting and making a judgement on what you hear, and on what you see. Like it or not, we do have our own perceptions, and we make judgements of people, perhaps too quickly, nevertheless it's an inevitable consequence of either two or more people coming together. You can't say whether you like somebody by what they write on a computer screen, as there is no real intonation in the words so the personal interaction is still important. Sitting at home, hour after hour, in front of a computer, is an isolating, lonely experience—people need people. The internet is an amazing tool, but it mustn't become a substitute for personal interaction, but the danger is, that it will—in fact, it already has.

More and more people are shopping online. This can be a helpful tool, because you're able to view the things you buy in the comfort of your own home, without being pushed and shoved by others, but there's still nothing like a bit of retail therapy, going around the shops, picking up the atmosphere, with the noise and the smells, and the interaction between people in the stores, although, it has to be said, sadly, not always polite! Nevertheless, to physically make the effort, to get yourself ready, and go out is very important. I wonder if, in years to come, there will be more incidents of agoraphobia because people are losing the will to go out, and are becoming more fearful.

There's a world out there, and we must help our loved ones live it. The computer can be a good source of sharing, but it can also be a source of segregating people, of losing the family interplay. Gone are the days, it seems, when the average family sit around the kitchen table, having their evening meal and sharing the issues of the day. Now, it's a meal put on a tray, taken up to the bedroom and eaten in front of the computer, that's not good for family relationships— whatever happened to the good old Sunday roast which was shared together without our mobile phones beeping? Is this a case for going back to the old-fashioned way of doing things just a little? The world is not going to shut down if we are away from the computer or mobile phone for half an hour; in fact, I think it would do our brain the power of good if we could give it a rest.

A thought:

The wonderful revelation about the internet is that it can open up a whole new world for people of all ages. There are more and more silver surfers, those elderly people who have found the internet, and had the courage to grapple with all things new for them, and delighting in what they can discover on all kinds of fascinating websites. Sadly, there are those out there who don't have this feel-good factor, and want to corrupt websites and the minds of some people sitting in front of their computer screens. We have to be ever mindful making sure we only use this wonderful technology for good.

I know of many people who use their mobile phones and computers for prayer groups and supporting others on a spiritual level. This is the use of the internet in a very productive way. Wouldn't it be great if we could help the Christian faith grow stronger by this means?

A prayer:

Lord, there are many people who are sitting in front of a computer screen because they are lonely, and have lost the art of making friends. Help them to realise that friendship won't happen unless they get out into the wider world and don't let the internet be a substitute for sharing and getting to know someone. The church can be a great source of new friends with a common ground. Lord, let the internet be a power for good and not evil. When people have the skills, and they can see things going wrong and issues that should be reported, give them the courage to take that step, making them proud that they have stopped wrongdoing.

Let the internet be a place where so many people are helped, let it be a place of discovery, of wonderment and interest, and let it be a place where we can find new skills, new modes of employment, along with the opportunity for romantic entanglements. The internet makes us used to getting an instant response. With You, Lord, we don't always get an instant answer, nor in the form that we expect. We try to make it all come right too quickly. You want us to work it out for ourselves. Speaking to You, Lord, we work through our issues. We may not discover Your answer immediately, but in time, Your will for us will be revealed.

Teenage Friendships

As an adult, it's hard to remember what it was like when you were a teenager, it seems that too many years have gone by. I can remember many times when I wanted the floor to open up and swallow me, when parents and relations teased unmercifully and I went red in the face and wanted to hide, but there was nowhere to go.

It's horrendous when people belittle a view and speak as though your opinion counts for nothing. In the end, all that happens is that your confidence is shattered, you believe that everyone will view your opinion as stupid. The thought of meeting new people, rather than being a pleasure, becomes a trauma. How do we break down this barrier? The first rule of thumb is to say, 'I don't have to apologise for being in this world, I'm me—what you see is what you get!' Then as you meet someone for the first time, don't regard them as a threat, but as a potential new friend. If we approach someone in friendship, especially with a smile, then the barriers will come down. Sometimes it's hard to fathom what makes one person attracted to another, it's not just about the latest clothes, perfume, make-up or mobile phone, these images that we present to the world are only skin deep. It's difficult in the early stages of friendship to really judge how quickly you should develop it—jump in too soon and it can be destroyed forever, take too long and people will have a totally different opinion of you. How do we strike that balance?

The friendships that we make may last for years, your friends may see you through thick and thin, good times and bad, celebrate with you and weep with you. Those friendships are really special. It's hard to know what constitutes a special friendship, in fact, I suppose it's almost impossible to define. Yet, when it happens, it's beautiful; you know when it's special because it's effortless. Even when one of you is absent and after months you come together again, you can often pick up where you left off, as though the week and months, or in some cases, years, had stood still. There's an ease about the relationship and usually laughter, teasing and rapport, which is unique to you both.

Today, many people have friends of both sexes and they are comfortable with that arrangement. We don't start out by assuming that every friendship will turn into a physical relationship. All too often, the physical relationship isn't regarded as special. It's something that just happens between friends. Yet a coming together of minds and bodies is a very special gift given to each one of us.

The issue that will really matter is integrity, respect and loving concern for another human being. If we believe that love is just about gratification and satisfying our feelings, then it tells us is that we don't have enough respect for another human being, or indeed respect for ourselves. Our body and what we do with it is a gift, given to us by God, it may only be an outer casing that the world sees, but it's important that we use it lovingly and wisely.

A thought:

When we are confident and comfortable in the friendship, we're then at ease with ourselves, and in being at ease we experience a level of harmony. Our relationship with God, if it's working well, is like a comfortable friendship, where we can talk to him and know that we'll be shown the way forward.

A prayer:

Lord, when we come to you and we get familiar you are like a trusted friend, so much a part of our life. You're always there but we might drift in and out, depending on our mood. We know that we can depend on you to strengthen, support and guide. It's incredible how you answer our prayer in so many ways, if we can only keep our eyes and ears open to the world around us. We can never truly keep our friendship if we constantly say to our friends that we don't have time. Just like our relationship with You, we have to make time and be still in this noisy world of ours to hear what You're saying. Help us be open to You in friendship, and be thankful.

Exam Results

The weeks and months leading up to examinations, for whatever level or grade they happen to be, are incredibly tense for all concerned. There are those terrible feelings of doubt and inadequacy, which many experience when swotting for an exam, which does not seem to be going well. The pacing up and down as we try to remember facts that won't always go in, and those anxious times when we look back at past examination papers to see what issues haven't come up in the last few years, in the hope that we can soak the right facts into our brain like a sponge. And, please God, get a good result!

Parents are crucial at this time to give a friendly word, a hot drink and a meal, and a change of scene for a while, but they are also there to give reassurance, and to say that as long as we've done our best, then they will support us, whatever the result. This is a very vital prop when we're preparing for an exam.

For some, that all important pass, however hard they try, may not be obtainable. They feel guilty that somehow they have failed, and failed their parents. They feel that not to have a place at university is a disaster; it may be that the academic path is not the right one for them, and for some a practical career using people or creative skills may be just what's needed. A good exam result should be the passport to a new way of life, a way of opening up the mind to explore new things, make new friends, and hopefully put you on the path for a future career that will give you much satisfaction and many challenges.

No one knows when they start on the academic journey, where it'll take them. Often, people change courses halfway through and take their life into a totally different direction from where they thought it would go. They may suddenly realise that the course they had set their heart on was not for them. There's no shame in trying and failing, the shame is in not trying at all.

I can remember all too well the morning of an exam, where I felt hot and bothered, and it was as though I had a brick in my stomach and couldn't eat. The thought of breakfast was horrifying. When I went into the examination room and was told to turn the paper over and read the questions, my mind went into a panic. I looked at the paper and, at first glance, thought I can't answer any of these… What on earth am I going to do?

Just concentrate, don't look at the whole paper. Just think of one question that you feel you could have a good stab at. Once you get started, you then calm down and realise that you might be able to answer another question on the sheet; before you know it, the invigilator will call time and you'll have completed your paper anyhow.

I had a simple rule of thumb—I never studied the night before an exam. The day before I looked at past papers and swotted up on the subjects that hadn't been used for several years, I also did this just before the examination started. I can remember, when I did my preaching exams, that I struck lucky and had the very subject that I had worked on that morning, it really was God working. Examination over, our fate is in the hands of someone else, waiting for that little brown envelope to drop through the letterbox on a certain day is a nail-biting experience.

I can remember shaking as I tore open the envelope, and being overjoyed when the result was good. There were celebrations then alright! That was the time when I felt for my parents and family. How would they feel if it all went pear-shaped? I knew that they would be there picking up the pieces, if it were necessary, but also there to join in the joyous celebration of passing.

As for the future, we can't say what will happen; we can only live for now, this is just one more step along the way.

A thought:

When we go into a panic about our exams, worrying ourselves sick because we need a certain grade, and fretting that we might not get it, we have to ask ourselves the question why are we getting so fretful? There's always the opportunity of a retake. As long as we know we did our level best then we have nothing to reproach ourselves for. So often, we study certain subjects and they become so much a part of our life that they become part of us, then, in later years, we find that we've never used the material that we learnt for examinations. Yet, we survived and whatever the result, good or bad, we'll still survive.

Examinations in themselves do not mean a great deal in the general scheme of things, within our daily life, what they prove is that we have the ability to learn, and take in facts, and write a reasonable discussion paper on a given subject. They're not the be all and end all of our life; they are just a very small part of it.

A prayer:

Lord, for all those working towards their examination, or finals, give them the resolve to keep going. Steel them from the overwhelming anxiety that can stultify their brain, making it impossible for facts to go in and stay there. Lord, keep them well, keep them focused, but, more importantly, keep them happy. No exam is worth being overwhelmed or overburdened with, life will go on. Help them know that their loved ones are with them, their friends are so often in the same boat. If, when they receive the envelope, it isn't the prize that they were hoping for, give them the courage to take the disappointment and begin again, knowing that, whatever happens, You're with them, and if a change of direction is called for, You will be there helping them determine what they should do.

Going to University

Those examination passes are the passport to greater things, a sense in which we suddenly realise our own worth. Looking round at university places and colleges, deciding what courses you want to do, is an exciting, yet scary, time.

Having made the choice, there's all the preparation for going to uni and coping for the first time in a hall of residence by yourself. Mum and Dad are no longer there to prop you up, or provide that clean shirt just when you need it, and it's hard to prioritise. The choice between a pint of beer or a glass of wine with your new friends versus beans on toast, because you haven't any money, is a hard one to make. It's surprising how, when finances are tight, vegetarian food is often the best option!

Holding down a part-time job and studying can often be a tricky balancing act. For the first time in your life you suddenly find yourself in the unenviable position of worrying about budgets, yet it's a brilliant learning curve. The cost of university tuition, and other supplementary charges, is an incredibly daunting prospect, especially when students come from a financially poorer background. Many who have the ability for academia may think twice because of the financial burden, and this is a tragedy.

At this time, friends and family are really vital to give a sense of continuity and balance. It's quite frightening, stepping out into the world of academia, but it's even harder to admit that you're scared; so, it's crucial that help is at hand. It's a wonderful time to discover how the academic world expands the mind, and makes us think in a much more expansive way, showing us the great holes in our knowledge, sending us down all sorts of tangents and different pathways that we hadn't previously imagined, illuminating our minds even more. I don't know if university education is the be all and end all of everything, but what it teaches is the ability to think, to think critically, and, more importantly, the ability to think for yourself.

Whilst you are growing and your mind is expanding in all directions, Mum and Dad are at home carrying on with the day-to-day tasks. When you've relied on your parents for so many things, it's hard for them to let go. Parents can often be forgotten in this process. They're not just there to carry belongings backwards and forwards to uni, it's worth remembering that they need contact too. It's a chance, however, for the parents to get part of their own individuality back, and have some special time, that's private to them, helping them to get in touch with each other again.

Three years is a long time in which there will be many joys, but there will also be many ups and downs, especially when it comes to final examinations, and the hard work that has to be put in whilst you create your thesis. If you can have a goal, a vision of where you want your life to be in three years' time, at the start of your university education, then you'll have done well. The day you put on the cap and gown, and receive your academic scroll, is a day for you to be proud of. That pride isn't just for you, but for your family and friends also, who have shared this time with you, make it a day that you'll always remember.

Education is a very precious gift that we're given. It isn't just about tuition fees and grants, it's about becoming a whole person, fully rounded in your thinking, ready to meet the challenges of the world outside of academia.

A thought:

Don't allow yourself to be so fearful that you can't grasp the opportunities with both hands. Going to university or college is a time for striking out, finding your feet, being independent and, hopefully, shaping the person that you'll become in adulthood. It's a time for experimentation, by that I don't mean drugs, I mean discovering what's out there that makes you think, freeing your mind. Knowledge can be explosive, but it can also be the very thing that takes you away from family roots. It's hard to hold onto the things that were so much a part of your general life. You're at the stage when you want to jettison everything and begin again, but remember that when you're moving on with your new life, your loved ones are still at home.

A prayer:

Lord, as we face the challenge of going to university, preparing to leave home, help us really appreciate the opportunity that we've been given. Help us not to waste this time, but value every God-given second, help us to develop a work ethic, give us "stickability". Help us not to take the easy way out, of socialising with our friends, when we've work to do. Make us worthy of the task ahead, and help us to be thankful and rejoice in our achievements when we are successful.

Finding Work

There's so much negativity around the whole process of finding employment. The media have much to answer for here. The way they talk down the job market, expressing no real optimism for our young people fresh out of university, excited by the challenges of life, is wrong. There's always work out there if we're prepared to get off our backsides, and show that we're willing to put the effort in for the reward.

In the beginning, it may not be the work that we trained for, or indeed hoped for, but it's work nevertheless, and the harsh reality is that we have to keep the wolf from the door. Working gives us a sense of pride and well-being, there's nothing worse than sitting around waiting for the day to go. You have to have a plan of action when you get up in the morning, particularly when you're writing job applications, it's all about self-belief and selling yourself. If you don't start by believing in yourself, then nobody else is going to, you have to make that prospective employer feel that when he or she reads your application, you stand out from all the rest.

Don't go at this task half-heartedly, believing that it's a waste of time and pointless. Go at it with the view that you'll get this job (and if not this one, another), and never miss the opportunity to speak to people about what you want to do. You never know how a chance conversation might give you the very break that you're looking for.

Think of yourself as a sales person, only this time you're selling yourself. Make your applications not only reflect your academic qualifications, but make that letter show a more rounded view of who you really are—your hobbies and interests and so on. There are jobs out there but perhaps, in the beginning, don't set your sights too high, it may be necessary to work up to what you want. Use your creative mind, think about what needs to be done, where the gaps are, where the niche market is, and try and plug it. Many entrepreneurs started with nothing, but they had a seed of an idea which they planted and made it grow—you can do the same.

I say this as a person who has pursued and succeeded in five different careers and at the time of writing this piece, I have worked for fifty-three years without a break. Not a bad achievement in a world that's so tenuous on the job front. The real answer is, don't give up, just keep on keeping on, until you're successful.

A thought:

Developments, such as job clubs, support from organisations such as Jobcentre Plus, with its opportunities for retraining, are wonderful and there should be many more of them, and much more help at hand. At the end of the day, all the jobcentres and clubs in the world cannot actually make you a member of the workforce, there's only one person who can do that, and that's you. You have to be fit for purpose, to use the modern phrase, and if that means further study in the evenings to reach your goal, then go ahead and do it. Keep yourself mentally and physically focused and active, don't stagnate in front of the television or DVD, get out there.

Be in the world and truly live it, and, if you can't find paid work, then do something to help somebody else that will give you a great sense of self-worth and satisfaction, and may help you to change direction, if you feel that the path you've already gone down is not right for you.

It's all about testing the water, developing wholeness within yourself, and realising your own strengths. Sometimes, in the quagmire of family life and study, our own strengths can get lost amongst what other people tell us we should be doing, or the assumptions others make about us. It can be hard to keep your head above water and strike out for your own identity—this is your chance. You could be on the threshold of something really important, don't lose the opportunity by being apathetic.

A prayer:

Lord, help us to keep focused. When an unsuccessful application letter drops through the letterbox, help us not to feel defeated by the task ahead. Help us to have the courage to revisit the style of our application, and see how we can change it in a way that best shows ourselves. Help us not to aim too high, and not be too proud to take a more menial job whilst we wait for an opportunity to come up. Help us to be aware of our appearance, the way we behave and our social manners, so that we can make a prospective employer want us as part of his or her workforce. Help us to be proud of our achievements, and go in there with our eyes open, looking towards You, and Your teaching, which will enhance our future life.

Pegging Your Dirty Linen to the Line

I'm sure we can all remember what it was like when we were little, when we were told to keep a secret, not to breathe a word about our brother or sister's birthday present, or some other family event that was meant to be a surprise. If it was good, we were eager to share it with other family members or friends, we would almost get to the point of bursting before the great day arrived! It's okay when you're little if you spill the beans, but it's not okay when you're an adult.

The criterion is when someone says something to you that is of a sensitive nature, then the rule of thumb would be to keep it to yourself. No one wants to have the reputation of being the kind of person that spreads news, good or bad, like wildfire. The only person who should peg out your dirty linen is yourself, if you're the kind of person that can be trusted with somebody's feelings, then you'll quickly get a reputation for this.

I know some people can be super-sensitive in this regard, wanting to keep everything so close to their chest that it's as though they're in a suit of armour, but that's their choice. People go for counselling because they know that the counsellor will have heard many variations on a similar theme, yet the dirty linen and the difficult bits of people's lives are left in the counselling room, the issues don't go any further. The therapeutic reason for counselling is that the client leaves their problems in the counselling room and walks away, hopefully, with a lighter heart. The old saying, 'A trouble shared is a trouble halved,' is only true when you can trust the person you're sharing it with. It could be that a trouble shared may be a trouble multiplied if you're not careful, so if you want someone to keep something confidential, then you should make that absolutely clear.

It's all about choosing your confidantes wisely, so that you can be free to make choices and change. There's nothing to be gained by spreading useless gossip. If you find it difficult to trust, but you need to offload, perhaps the most likely place to do that will be in a house of prayer. When the relationship you have with God is good and you can regard him like a trusted Father then it's an enormous privilege, for he is the Father who will not be judgemental, he is the Father who will be accepting of you. You know what the church teaches, you know what the Bible teaches and what Jesus's interpretation of it was. Jesus did not stick to the letter of the law, rather he lived by his principles, and he certainly didn't condemn or cast the first stone.

Christ had a particular way of making those who felt smug about their life stand back from it and reflect. We all need to do this from time to time. None of us know how our life can suddenly change, or what our circumstances might be, or whether we might fall from grace. We can only live our life as we see fit, but when we live it according to Christian values then hopefully, we'll stay on the right path.

The true answer is, that when we look at the teachings of Christ, never once did he condemn people, he supported them, gave them loving touch and much human contact. He told them that for their life to change, they had to change—it's a lesson to us all. The old way may not be working, so we have to come to God in humility and weakness, knowing that we'll be strengthened to live our life in the Christian way, and thereby be godlier. That may seem a very strange concept in today's world, so many people are just out for themselves and they don't care who they tread on to get there. All the time we have to try and say, 'If Christ were in this situation, what would he do and how would he act?'

The tittle-tattling is extremely harmful. There are those situations when a person knows that if they want something spread around, but they don't have the courage to do it themselves, they will tell certain people knowing that it will go out on the bush telegraph! The local village shop may be a great source of broadcasting in this regard, so remember, when you feel the urge to spread the word, unless it's the teaching of Christ, keep quiet.

A thought:

My mum used to say, 'If you can't say anything good about someone, don't say anything at all.' This is a very useful maxim. If we adopt the attitude of spreading kind words instead of hateful ones, then the world would be a far happier and nicer place. It would also be a more positive place because people would be much happier. Try it for a day, then for a week, then a month and so on until you have completed a whole year. Then, step back and realise how you have changed!

A prayer:

Lord, when we come to You because we're troubled in body, mind or spirit; help us to know that You're there openly to receive us and willing to accept us, with all our faults and failings. You know the fragility of the human spirit and the human condition, but You love us unconditionally. You taught Your Son to say, 'Father, forgive them.' When we say or do the wrong thing, help those people concerned to find it in their hearts to forgive us and help us to have the courage to admit that we were wrong.

Bringing the
Boyfriend/Girlfriend Home

After those early teenage years comes the development of forming lasting relationships. It's a very anxious time for the young person when they bring the new boyfriend or girlfriend home to meet Mum and Dad. They worry about the difficult things that they might say, or that Mum and Dad might embarrass them by bringing out the early photographs. Or telling their new partner what they were like when they were little. It's also a time when they feel under scrutiny, when they're being watched carefully by the respective parents. This may not be the final relationship, it may be the start of many, but it's the time of discovering, not only about sexuality, but about their own personal behaviour and how they will treat others.

It's a time that parents have often forgotten. Surely if they think back they too can remember those embarrassing moments, the time when they wanted the floor to open up and swallow them. It's also a time when the young couple can express love's young dream to one another, it's the intensity of that first relationship that is so special. We can always remember our first love, by that I don't just mean a one-night stand, but a genuine relationship that, although it may not have lasted, was very meaningful at the time.

I can also remember what it was like when that first relationship broke down, and I felt that my world had come to an end. When that happens, we need parents and loved ones around us, not to make us feel silly and small, and insignificant, but to recognise the pain, and help us to begin again. Help us to learn to value ourselves and realise that there are plenty more fish in the sea. When you're young and in love, it's hard to realise that there are plenty more people to choose from, yet it's important to regroup and begin again.

A thought:

When young people are discovering each other and their own sexual identity, it's often the time when they need someone outside the family unit to befriend them, and support them. This is why agony columns in newspapers and magazines play such a useful role in this regard. Often they will scour the pages to see if anyone is coming up with the kind of questions they want to ask, because they don't have the courage to put their needs out there.

It's also the time when friends and loved ones are essential.

A prayer:

Lord, when young people take the first huge step to adulthood by forming their first true relationship, help them not just to see it in terms of sexual gratification, but for it to be a time of discovery, a time of respecting another human being and forming friendships that they hope will last, but recognise that perhaps they may not. Whatever happens between the young couple, let it be a time of happiness and enjoyment, for which they can be forever thankful.

Acceptance of Your Child's Partner

It's never easy, from the parental point of view, when your child makes their choice as to who they want to spend the rest of their life with. Parents, mothers in particular, often feel that no one could match up to them. They will undoubtedly make comparisons and, try as they may not to find fault, they frequently do. This, I suppose, is all part of the natural processes of growing up, and growing away, from one's parents, but it's often a very painful process.

We frequently forget that it wasn't so long ago when we made choices—choices that members of our family wouldn't have made. They see our relationship from a distance, and are able to stand back and watch. Sometimes it's not that the chosen partner is difficult, it's just that they're different from the image that Mum had in her mind for that nice homely wife or husband. Perhaps, in the end, it may be found that the choice that their child made was the wrong choice, but they have to be free to explore what's right for them, and the partner has to be given a chance. There's nothing worse than feeling unaccepted, and therefore unloved.

Times are changing—generations, attitudes, and morals have changed. I frequently find myself saying, 'When I was younger…' or 'It wasn't like this in my day…' I think we're now living in a very sad and, by and large, selfish world, the must-have-it-now culture and the wanting-to-get-rich culture, doesn't help the sense of integrity, morals and a good, clean and healthy lifestyle. If we want to be different and stand out from the crowd, then to many we are regarded as odd, and this is sad.

So how do young people starting out in life strike out for their own identity? Stamping their own particular lifestyle preferences on their relationship? It might not be what parents wanted or expected, but, at the end of the day, it's nothing to do with them. When parents are constantly critical, creating atmospheres, it does nothing for overall public relations. We need to try and get along with each other in life, because we only have one chance. No one wants to feel unwanted, worst of all they don't want the feeling that they're being scrutinised at every turn. They must be free to be themselves, a free spirit who can express their love in whatever way they choose.

It's all about not trying to put an old head on young shoulders, let the young be young, let them make mistakes and choices, even if they turn out to be the wrong ones. This is how people develop and grow. No one can wrap their child up in cotton wool, protecting them from the painful things of life; life is all about taking risk, and grabbing opportunities with both hands. Our role, as adults, looking in from the sidelines, is to enjoy being around young people, and embrace them for who, and for what, they are.

Hopefully, they'll be parents themselves one day and they will go through the same emotional turmoil and tension with their own child. It's at that point that they will discover your tensions and misgivings, but hopefully, it's also a time when they'll make a lasting, bonding friendship with the son or daughter-in-law.

A thought:

It has been my experience that the more parents express their opinions on the boyfriends or girlfriends of their children, the more their children will dig their heels in and be ever determined to make their own choices. This is, very definitely, a no-win situation; the better part of valour is to wait until their child goes to them and asks their opinion. The danger is that the parents may say too much, always be mindful that your opinion may come back to haunt you in later life. Comments made by parents are never forgotten by their children, especially in relation to a partner.

A prayer:

Lord, when someone new comes into the family it can feel quite threatening for parents, because, for the first time, their way of doing things may be scrutinised and challenged. This is a tough time for all concerned, so I ask Your blessing upon the family. I ask that there may be realism, and give and take. Having a good relationship is not a one-way ticket; it should be a time where both sides freely share.

Lord, help the parents not to be too critical. Help them to realise that they were young once and that love can often be blind. Help them not to put their ideals into the mind of the son or daughter, giving their opinion on who, or what, makes a good partner. Let the young couple have enough freedom to grow together in love and friendship, so that there will be a real sense of togetherness in future life.

Holidays

My view of family holidays is probably very different from what some of you have experienced. Being born in 1950, and coming from the East End of London, from a working class background, there wasn't very much money around for exotic holidays. However, I would count myself amongst one of the lucky ones because Mum and Dad worked hard to give their three children the very best that they could. Because of my disability they thought it was important for me to get away from the grimy streets of London, and have some sea air to strengthen my lungs and make me physically stronger.

So it was decided to buy a caravan and place it on a site at Seasalter near Whistable in Kent. This was our means of holiday from the age of seven to twenty-seven, and I must admit, although I appreciated the Kent coastal resorts, I reached the point where I never wanted to see them ever again. There was a wider world out there, and I wanted to experience it, but my dad loved the sea and loved what he knew, and the friends he made, and never wanted to change or go anywhere else.

That aside, the sea was literally across the road from our campsite. It used to be lovely sitting up on the sea wall watching the tide coming in, with boats appearing in the murky distance. The beach was full of soft sand, pebbles and sea shells and we had lots of fun selecting different coloured shells and making things from them. When finances were better, Dad built his own boat and later obtained a speedboat. We had much fun crossing to the Isle of Sheppey and going out fishing from the boat. All healthy, natural pursuits, but when I grew up, I wanted to go further afield.

I spent many happy holidays in the West Country, staying with my music teacher's family at Portishead in Bristol. We visited Weston-Super-Mare, Yeovil, Bath, the Mendips, Cheddar Gorge and many wonderful places in the West Country, that gave me the desire to explore places around Britain.

Holidays are what you make of them—they're our own personal oasis in a very busy world, but they are the stuff that hopes and dreams are made of. Whether they are basic holidays, like mine, or wonderfully exciting ones such as Disneyworld, Egypt or Australia, they are our sense of aspiration, our goals, and the things we want to strive for. They are the places we want to see and things we want to experience, such as food from other cultures and exploring the world as we go.

A thought:

All of our lives would be poorer if we couldn't go on holiday. All of us must have something to strive for, to look forward to, and to know that we're going to have new vistas to see and new delights for our senses. Without them, we would be emotionally bereft—we need a sense of recharging our batteries.

Holidays are not just about our needs, but the needs of those we share our life with. They can also be a source of tension when we're not used to spending two weeks, or more, with someone, so it can also be a learning curve in how we dissipate tensions and make it a happy time.

A prayer:

Lord, help us to appreciate the interludes from the daily work routine. Help us to plan where we want to go, places we want to explore, and appreciate them. Help us to have a sense of wonderment and marvel at the countryside, buildings and architecture in other lands and help us to appreciate people from cultures other than our own. So often we'll see places that haven't been developed as our own country has, people who haven't had the same opportunities that we have had.

Help us to be thankful for what we have, that we have sufficient money to visit faraway places, enabling us to recognise that the world that we know, full of its materialism, is not always the better world. Often, people who have much less than we have can teach us very powerful lessons about true value, and what really creates happiness. Help us to realise that the candyfloss world that we live in on holiday isn't how we would wish to live for the rest of our lives.

Marriage Breakdown

When two people marry, there's much expectation. In the early part of the relationship, there's communication, the sense in which the couple readily check out with one another what each of them want. Sadly, with the passing of time and the pressures of life, this constant communication drifts off, and suddenly the couple find themselves doing their own thing, living their own life, making their own decisions, rather than sharing with one another. This is the danger time when the relationship often breaks down. It's partly due to the assumptions that we make when our partner becomes so familiar, and we think we know what they want, rather than asking what they want.

It's the time when marriages drift apart, and people seek solace elsewhere. For those who find a new relationship, they are often happy; if they weren't, there wouldn't be any point in doing it. It's those who are left bereft and hurting that I feel concerned about, those who are watching on the sidelines, seeing the arguments, the stress and the hurt that the couple are causing to one another. It's often tough on those who are watching, especially if the people watching are young children, then the wrangling starts, all the logistical problems of breaking up a home, and beginning again. Often, the young children are not aware of just how stressful the situation becomes, until they themselves may become the reason for the arguments between their parents.

What's worse is when the new partner comes onto the scene, and there's someone important in Mum or Dad's life. It's difficult for a child to come to terms with this new person in place of Mum or Dad in the house. This may be new and fulfilling to their parent, but to the child, who looks on, it's confusing. There needs to be much more time given to building a relationship and creating rapport with the children, letting them set the pace, so that the life that they share with this new person is happy and comfortable, the child will make comments when they have adjusted to this situation.

Push it too quickly, and the child will feel hurt and rejected for someone new. We can't force children to like our new partner, they can't be bribed into acceptance—nor should they be. This change should be done lovingly, caringly and in a nurturing way. Children shouldn't be used in a manipulative sense, because they are now in a difficult position over divided loyalty. Tug-of-love wars are not clever if you're in the middle of them, it's so hard for a child who loves both parents to make the decision as to where they should live, and who should be their main parent during the week.

Some might say that for the roles to be divided in this way can be advantageous, because the child gets two sets of parents instead of one. That's fine if the relationship is happy and healthy. It's tough enough for a child to have to go into another family setup, but it's even tougher when they return home, perhaps having had a lovely time, only to have it shot down in flames by the constant barrage of questions. How do they deal with the feelings of divided loyalty and the stress of the parent back home? This family transition should be dealt with as gently and amicably as possible.

It's also a time to think of the grandparents, who have formed relationships with their daughter or son's partner, and of course a loving relationship with their grandchildren. So often, when the family breaks up, it's the grandparents who suffer; they are left with their feelings unresolved. They have always been there for their grandchildren, and they have loved them through every stage, now, due to family break-up and anger, one side or the other wants to keep the children away from the original grandparents because they don't want a reminder of the previous life.

So the grandparents are left high and dry, trying to have a relationship with their grandchildren, which frequently is rejected, leaving the grandparents to feel hurt. It's terrible when we use people like pawns on a chessboard, those involved on the sidelines didn't choose to be dragged into this situation, but now they find themselves stuck. It's important to remember that they can't turn their love on and off like a tap.

A thought:

The break-up of family life, when it comes, is terrible regardless of the cause. What matters are the consequences for those involved. Before it gets to this stage, let the couple concerned genuinely seek counselling and mediation in whatever form is helpful, so that everything possible can be done to prevent this difficult situation.

A prayer:

Lord, when marriage breaks down let it not be a time when the couple score points against one another. Let it be a time of genuinely trying to find out the reasons why things went wrong. May the couple do all they can to seek reconciliation and begin again. Sometimes when a couple go for counselling, it shows the difficulties in their true light, so, if it's felt that the couple should separate, let it be done in a civilised way. Help the couple and all those who love them to be aware that each can play their part. May the children not be used like a game of tug-of-war, first being pulled one way, and then the other.

It's important, Lord, that the children feel safe. Be with them as they ask difficult questions as to why mummy and daddy are breaking up. Don't let them have feelings that they were rejected. Help the parents to heal those wounds, not only for themselves, but of their children and give them the patience to be loving, kind and nurturing, at a time when the children feel most vulnerable.

Mid-Life Crisis

Whenever people talk about the mid-life crisis, there'll be those who make jokes, some of these can be humorous, but to the person experiencing it, it's anything but funny. It really is the time when people take stock, usually between forty and fifty. Often, we feel like this when our life has become stuck and we feel as though our feet are in a pot of glue; there's no sense of direction and no sense of where we're actually heading.

Life has become somewhat boring, and this feeling is often transferred into our workplace and into our personal relationships. It's the time to rethink; it's not necessarily the time to find gimmicky ways of spicing up your relationship, however, it is the time to re-evaluate and appreciate your partner. All too often, the little things have been forgotten, the unexpected bouquet of flowers, or box of chocolates, given for no other reason than you want to let the person know that you care about them.

Marriage and relationships are all about working at it. It's a job in the true sense of the word, and it's a team effort. I've said many times, that it's all about communication; mid-life crisis can be overcome if you sit down and openly share your fears, some of which may be about changing direction, but also preparing for the future and getting one's house in order.

If there are causes which make the person unhappy, then they're not going to go away by sweeping them under the carpet. They must be talked about and freely shared and, in my view, given over to God. The mid-life thing only becomes a crisis if we let it, it should be the time when children have flown the nest and a couple are free to enjoy each other's company, in whatever way they choose. It may be the time to find a hobby that they can jointly share, a newfound enthusiasm for a particular skill or sport—anything that creates interest and makes you feel it's worth getting up in the morning, and good to be alive.

If these sentiments cannot be felt, and that depressive feeling of hopelessness remains, then perhaps it's time to seek the help of a counsellor or a GP, who may find reasons for that depression. I've seen many people as a counsellor who have, and are, suffering from an identity crisis because that is what this is really about. If we can identify the difficulties and try to change, then hopefully this mid-life crisis won't be a time of disaster, but a time of regrouping and preparing for the next phase of life, which is just as important as all the others—perhaps, in many ways, more so, because what changes you make now will affect your future life in retirement and beyond.

A thought:

Why do we trouble ourselves so much about the so-called mid-life crisis? We've reached that halfway point in our lives, although who can truly say what a halfway point is, as we never know what is going to happen to us, or how long we will live. It should be a time for celebration and rejoicing, that we've reached this point and come to no harm. It's also the time when we should re-evaluate our life, think about where we're going, and what we want to do, and also think about what we can do for others, or the environment in which we live. Life is not just for the taking, but also the giving.

A prayer:

Lord, when we're stuck in our emotions, when we feel that our life has no purpose, help us to see, through You, that You have given us a very special gift; a gift that's not ours to waste but to be used responsibly, lovingly, and carefully. The mid-life crisis is also a time of payback when we have to put something in to take something out. Lord, help us to see that our life is not just about material gain, but how we can prepare our life for the time that really matters, the time when we come face to face with You.

The time when we'll have to account for what we did in our life, rather than run away from it. At this point of the mid-life crisis, help us to mentally say to ourselves, 'I now have a second chance to put things right and move on.'

Keeping the Relationship Alive

It doesn't really matter whether I'm talking about the husband and wife, brothers and sisters, or relatives and friends; any relationship has to be a two-way process. If one person is doing all the giving, and the other, all the taking, it will never work, for any relationship to be successful, it takes mutual respect and consideration to keep it alive.

It's never the big things; it's the little things that are the most important. Remembering a birthday card, remembering to call when somebody is ill, or to congratulate them on a success, or an anniversary, and, most importantly, it's being there in times of trouble and stress.

For the married couple, it's about appreciation. When they are part of love's young dream they appreciate everything about one another—their favourite music, their smile and the look of love between them. As the years go on these acts of recognition and reconciliation, and growing in friendship, love and tolerance, between one another, somehow get lost in the quagmire of daily life. What do we do to change that? It's about remembering to tell someone that you love them, especially when they're going out and getting in their car, just in case they don't come back. It's about letting that person know how special they are and how precious you feel your life is together.

I can remember when I sat with my father by my mother's bed when she was unconscious in the intensive care ward. I said to my father: 'Mum can hear you, Dad, tell her that you love her.'

'She knows that,' was his response.

'Well, tell her anyway,' I insisted.

His response to her was, 'You were a good cook, mate, and you kept the house lovely and clean.'

I replied to him, 'Oh for God's sake, can't you do better than that?'

The real answer is that none of us truly know that we're loved, unless we're told, and unless there's good communication between the couple. So often, affection is a precursor to sex within a relationship, this I find is a great pity, because we should be able to give affection without sexual gratification at the end. It's those little things that matter, the recognition that your partner has been working so hard with family issues that they need a break, perhaps a weekend, quietly recharging their batteries, and being together, having time to say and do all the things that you want to.

In that way, you'll have a life where you lovingly grow old together, in appreciation of something beautiful and good, like a mature wine. Relationships should not be something that you can pick up and drop, like an old pair of shoes— relationships, especially those that are loving, have to be worked at.

A thought:

Never forget that the only time any of us have is now, you don't want to be saddled with the burden of the words 'If only I had done...' Don't have a life that is burdened by regret, have a life that is full, happy and enriched, and be thankful.

A prayer:

Lord, when we're with those that we love, help us to be thankful that they have enriched our life. Help us to cherish them, even when the relationship is difficult. When we have been together over the years, and shared so many issues, good and bad, and they have come with us through thick and thin, help us to be glad that they were there, walking with us, and, give us the courage to tell them how much it has meant to us that they were there by our side.

Lord, we thank You for their presence in our world that has influenced us in so many ways. Let the friendship we have shared be fulfilling. Marriage starts in friendship and deepens with love, may that deepening sense of valuing, one to the other, go on right to the end, and may we be ever thankful.

Preparing for the Future

When you have lead an active family life, with lots of comings and goings of your children, their friends, girlfriends, husbands or wives, and then the grandchildren, or even the greatgrandchildren, it's probably time to re-evaluate where you are, and think about the future. Perhaps there will be those of you who will say, 'I don't want to think about the future.' Understandable, yet there's nothing like forward planning, it saves an awful lot of heartbreak, stress and difficulty for your family members.

Forward planning isn't just about downsizing, but thinking of what kind of property you might wish for in later life when you aren't so mobile. What you could do twenty years ago is very different from what you can do now—the large garden that you always wanted may now be impossible due to infirmity, or if you can't deal with it yourself, it becomes a financial noose around your neck, because money has to be found to pay a gardener on a weekly basis. This can be difficult when funds have to be stretched.

So, the big house now becomes a bungalow, with a small but manageable garden. It's now the time to think about widening doorways and making the shower or bath more accessible, in case knee or hip replacements have to be done in the future. These adaptations are costly, also, they have to be thought about carefully, and the pieces of equipment chosen well. You may think that to speak in this way has a certain morbid quality to it, not so; this is being realistic and not sweeping the issues under the carpet. I hope and pray that all of us will have longevity, and a good quality of life, with lots of activity and friends, but for many of us, that won't be the reality.

Downsizing should mean that even after the adaptations you will have some finance to enable you to enjoy the latter stages of your life. At the end of the day, it's not about quantity of time, but quality of time. With the fear of the future taken away, you'll be free to enjoy yourself, for now is the time to find new pursuits. Perhaps, let the tour companies take the strain, visit places by coach or rail, rather than drive hundreds of miles, and relax, sit back, and let others worry for you, but enjoy the holidays nevertheless.

This is often the time when people have the experience of going on one of these all-inclusive cruises. Entertainment, food and wonderful scenery all provided in one fell swoop—what a treat! Go on, spoil yourself and make the most of your God-given life together.

A thought:

There will be those who will say there's nothing good about old age. I think they're wrong. Old age is fine if you have the opportunity to plan. Carefully look at what you might be able to do long before you reach it, have a plan of action, and find pursuits that you and your partner can mutually enjoy. More importantly, really enjoy the company of your children and grandchildren, making it an ever-open house. The more you welcome people in, the more they'll want to come back, then your old age won't seem nearly so lonely.

What you do now is an insurance policy for the future, enjoy the time you have to the full.

The one area that's so important is that the older generation has a great deal of experience on which others can draw. Often, they have the time to sit down with the younger generation, and give them an impression of years before they were born, which is a priceless gift.

A prayer:

Lord, it's often very hard for people who have had wonderfully active lives to think about their future life, which may not be so active. It's difficult when they may feel that their life is being controlled by other forces. Give them the courage and strength to grasp hold of this situation, and deal with it themselves, before events take them over. No one wants to lose control of their own life, so, wherever possible, it's important to forward plan.

Lord, those aspects of forward planning may be painful, for the elderly couple may be giving up many of the things they hold dear. Give them the strength to see downsizing as a new challenge, particularly if they move into a new area. Let them be happy in old age, and help them to know that they are loved and cared for through their knowledge and love of You.

Redundancy

When you've given much of your working life to one particular company and you're suddenly summoned to the manager's office, given a small envelope and told that they are very sorry but they'll have to make you redundant, it's profoundly shocking, not only to you, but your loved ones also.

There you were, thinking that your life was pretty much set, going along on an even keel. The kids are at school or college, half the mortgage is paid off, and you're comfortable in your own little niche.

Then you have to break the news at home. It's hard enough coping with it yourself, but to be the bearer of such tidings to someone you love is even harder. Once you're over the initial shock, it's a time for regrouping, a time to see where you are in the great scheme of things. Whether you can survive on the lump sum redundancy payment, or whether you're going to have to put yourself back on the job market in middle age, it's all quite hard to swallow.

Yet, it's also an opportunity to grasp. The sense in which you suddenly pull together and work as a team, determined not to be beaten by adversity, absolutely certain that, whatever happens, you'll win through, as long as you do it together. It may be the time when you look at retraining, or putting your redundancy into a business plan that has been formulating in your mind for a long time. It may be the time when the children realise that it's tough at home just now, they have to be more realistic with the demands that they make on Mum and Dad. They too will end up with different expectations, and they may well be for the better. An easy lifestyle can be a complacent one, but when life is hard, for whatever reason, it makes you take stock and re-evaluate, and that's no bad thing. That's something we all need to do from time to time, to really have a sense of where we're going in life.

I have known people who have said that when they were made redundant it was the best thing that ever happened to them. They changed direction and they really discovered what their marriage truly meant to them. Everything in life has a purpose and there are always two ways of looking at it— treating it as a total disaster, or as a God-given opportunity.

A thought:

Redundancy forces us to make life choices. Maybe it's the time when we realise that the big flash car and large family home don't necessarily bring happiness, but they do bring pressure to conform to the "norm", and the struggle to meet the household bills. Redundancy makes us revisit, and probably downsize, in our mind, a kind of individual cost-cutting exercise. During that cost-cutting, we discover the things that really matter; it isn't about having more and more possessions, and building bigger and better barns to put the possessions in, but instead, it helps us to focus on what are the more realistic options, but also helps us to grasp, and act on, new opportunities.

A prayer:

Lord, don't let the redundancy fill us with such fear and dread for the future that we're stultified by it. Help this news not to be the cause of more and more family discord, but let it be a sense in which we hold onto one another, and stick together through thick and thin, good times and bad. Help the person facing redundancy not to feel humiliated, or a failure, or let down. Help them keep their self-esteem. Help them, Lord, to have the courage to regroup themselves and rebuild, especially if it means branching out into something new. Let the branching out be a source of excitement and challenge and help them to know that You are there, holding their hand, all the way through.

Retirement

All of us find the prospect of retirement challenging, not least of all for the wives, husbands or partners at home. Retirement could be a golden opportunity, a chance when you can do those things that you have always wanted to do, whilst you're still fit and well, and able to enjoy them.

I had a friend who planned for retirement for herself and her husband from the very first week of their marriage. At the time, I found this rather strange, but now, some forty-five years on, I realise that this decision to prepare early for such an event was a marvellous thing to do. My friends had a wonderfully hectic life, but they have also had an extremely fulfilling retirement, travelling around the world, and going to many exotic places. They have also greatly enjoyed all the many experiences that they have shared together as a couple, it's like an insurance policy of memories for the future, when one of the partners are no longer here.

You may think that to plan in this way is a little morbid— not so, because my friends have had a wonderful time deciding where they'll go and what they'll do together, and I know it has enhanced their marriage a tremendous amount.

I can remember another friend who was really daunted by her husband's pending retirement. How would they get on? What would they do together? Would he get under her feet and drive her mad? She was really expressing fear about the loss of her independence and freedom. These issues were talked about between them, and carefully mulled over. Consequently, because they communicated, these anxieties never occurred, and they too have had a great retirement. Talking is the key!

Looked at in the right way, retirement can be such a freeing up of the mental processes, the opportunity to try new skills, learn a language, or have daily exercise, or do something such as buying a motor caravan and touring all around Britain. I can't think of anything more lovely to do, seeing all the sights of the English countryside, and having time to enjoy them to the full.

Some people approach their retirement with dread and apprehension, rather than joy. Don't just sit there, get out and do something, maybe give more time to your church, pastoral visiting voluntary work, and outreach. If we develop the right frame of mind, then I hope people will hear us say, 'I don't know how I found the time to work!' This is when retirement is healthy, productive, and good. This is when the couple make each other feel special and important, and that they really matter to each other.

If you have found communicating with your partner difficult because you don't know what makes them tick, or what really gives them pleasure, then retirement won't be easy, but if you see retirement as a joint venture then you'll have a different attitude towards it. Retirement is the reward for many years of hard work and struggle; it's the time when you now need to do something purely for yourself, and your own personal pleasure.

Some might say this is selfish. I don't think that that is the case at all—it's your personal reward for all the hard work over the years; enjoy it and be thankful.

A thought:

If we are not careful we can get bogged down by all the practicalities that we have to deal with regarding retirement. We can find ourselves in a quagmire of figures and finance, and the real opportunity that we're being given is lost. Forward planning and forward thinking is the key to coping with yet another stage in our lives. Retirement isn't the end, but a new beginning.

A prayer:

Lord, when retirement is offered, help us not to be full of trepidation. Help us to systematically work the issues through and make an informed choice. Help us to value the opportunity that we've been given, and make the most of every day. Help us to plan, to be excited by those plans, as children are over a holiday as it's important that we're happy about this newfound situation. More importantly, help us to be grateful that You're part of that retirement, walking with us and sharing it together.

Growing Old Together

I have a friend who used to be a marriage guidance counsellor. When talking about relationships of the older generation, she said in their youth, when they thought about their sexuality together, they climbed the peak of the highest mountain, now they are only climbing hillocks, but it doesn't matter on the height of the hill, what matters is that they're still climbing, this is true; Why do so many of the younger generation write relationships off when it comes to older people? Just because they are elderly, it doesn't mean that they have given up the power to love, just because they are elderly, it doesn't mean that they don't want the closeness of another human being, just because they are elderly, it doesn't mean that they've lost the ability to make a valid contribution in the world around them.

When new love comes in the mature stages of one's life, it's often very gentle and tender. They've had their excitement and maybe their fighting years earlier, now, often, all that they want is a peaceful co-existence, a good meal, a comfortable home and someone to cuddle up to and keep their feet warm at night. Soppy and sentimental? Bring it on!

There's nothing wrong with those qualities within a relationship. Many so-called elderly people still lead incredibly active lives, both on a physical and an emotional level. After all, who are we to determine what's right for another human being, they have to find their own position in life, and make the best of what they've got.

What is lovely in old age is that there are the memories of all the things that they did together, or with a previous partner. I know of one lady who married in her early seventies, she's really happy and leads an active life. Perhaps their children might frown, or even disapprove, if Mum or Dad meets somebody else and forms a relationship, but look at it positively; if they are happy and content, living their life to the full, then it takes the responsibility off their children's hands for a much longer period of time, and that's got to be good for all concerned.

Independence should be something that we fight for right to the end. After all, the simple things, such as what we will eat, what we will wear and how we will spend our money, on a daily basis, is fundamental to our very existence.

I know of elderly couples who buy themselves a timeshare where people can swap their dates with others in a similar organisation, and visit other countries. What an opportunity, what a way to extend your retirement, maybe through travelling you realise that you would like to learn a language, so that you can fully appreciate the countries that you like to visit, or join a choir, or learn to play a musical instrument— anything that exercises your brain, hands and lungs. Walking can also be another wonderful pursuit if you are mobile, because you see the countryside at a slower pace and appreciate its beauty.

It may be the very time that you find your creative, artistic self, through painting and other art forms, or perhaps in writing, it's whatever suits you, it's whatever keeps the pot boiling in terms of a relationship. It doesn't matter about age, whether you are seventeen or seventy, a relationship has to be worked on, and the advantage is that you will have a wealth of years on which to draw, and understand each other so well that you almost know how the other person thinks.

There is a danger that, if you're not careful, you'll assume too much, and not allow your partner to really be themselves—whatever that may mean.

Growing old gracefully can be a beautiful time, a time when you treasure the years for their own sake. You know that you have limited time so if you value what God has given, you'll make the most of it, and so, don't waste it.

A thought:

All too often in the past, we've written people off because they are old. The light has suddenly dawned in the realisation that elderly people have a wealth of experience, and we are foolish to reject them, and ignore them at our peril. The younger generation don't have all the answers and because so many elderly people have struggled through life due to the war years and such like, they have much that they can teach us about family values, and the appreciation of life.

Many were on the poverty line during the war because there wasn't enough food to go around. Now they can appreciate far more the lovely meal put in front of them. They were often extremely good managers of small budgets, because they had to eke out their earnings carefully. We take so much for granted, but we can learn so much from the elderly who stand on the sidelines and watch.

A prayer:

Lord, old age is a time for reflection, a time for remembering, a time for settling family difficulties, and trying to live in peace and harmony. Lord, I pray that those elderly people still fortunate enough to be together as a couple will grow ever closer in mutual respect, and love for one another. It will be, I hope, Lord, a time when they come to You, a time when they can look at Christian values and be thankful for them.

Lord, be with them as they make difficult decisions in their life, and help their life to be enhanced by the newfound joys that they have together. Let their children find them a blessing, and may they want to be with their elderly loved ones, resting in the knowledge that the limited years are now precious years and be thankful.

Role Reversal

Mum and Dad have been part of our existence all of our life. It's incredibly difficult when we've relied on them so much over the years, to see them as people who need help, rather than be the helpers. We're now in a situation of role reversal, which is incredibly hard for us to cope with especially when our dad, for example, has been physically strong and capable. Now, through age, he's frail and very weak, sometimes confused and dependent upon others, yet he wouldn't wish to admit it.

Dad still sees us as his children, where he's in control, calling the shots. Now it's a very different scenario; we're trying to help *him* sort *his* life out. It doesn't matter which parent you apply this scenario to, the consequence is the same. When one parent is suffering from dementia, or at the very least, confusion, it's hard to make sense of it all and one feels like banging one's head against the wall in trying to make them understand. We're not there to make things difficult, or deliberately take away their independence, we're trying to stop them injuring themselves, or being taken advantage of by others, yet they still want to keep control and its right and fitting that, wherever possible, they are allowed to do so.

How do we strike a happy medium and balance in this difficult situation? How do we make them see that we genuinely care about them and want to do all we can to help?

So often, our parents have struggled through the war years, they know the value of money and the struggle to save and keep it, they want to hold onto it, because money represents independence and power. They can't see that sometimes it's not in their best interest, and helping them through the quagmire of Social Services rules, regulations, and jargon, is a complete nightmare.

They can't see that their child is perhaps more aware of these things than they are, because to them we're still their child, even though we may have children, and even grandchildren, of our own. How do we hold onto loving them, and still see them as our parents, even though illness and old age may have transformed them into a shadow of their former self?

It's very hard to see through all these difficulties, and hold onto the love we once shared, but if we believe that everyone has the right to love, and to have the right to human dignity, we must do it, whatever the emotional cost.

A thought:

Thank God there are organisations such as Age Concern or the Alzheimer's Society who often help those elderly people who fall through the net of social care. Many will not see their loved ones for months on end, the ones who do are extremely lucky. Those who don't have the support they need should be helped by the more able in the community, we shouldn't be like the story of the Good Samaritan, where people pass by on the other side, and it was left to a stranger to meet the needs of someone who had been robbed and beaten.

Hopefully, our elderly people won't be in that situation, but they will have the deprivation of loneliness and solitude, many of us could do something about this by inviting an elderly neighbour in for a meal from time to time, to let them know that we care about them. There are some very good people out there, who are already doing this, networking, supporting, and nurturing in the way that God would expect. Let's hope and pray that the community will be a community in the wider sense of the word, and practice what they know God teaches.

A prayer:

Lord, it's very hard for someone reaching the twilight of their years to come to terms with what's happening to them. No one wants to face old age and infirmity, but Lord, we pray that there will be people who will support them through this difficult time.

You will help those going through this period to know that they are welcome by someone else into their home. Lord, when we lead busy and active lives, we don't always understand the fear of loneliness. Help those people not to be afraid, but put their trust in You, that help will be at hand to make a difference in their daily lives.

Care Home

Sadly, the natural follow-on from the previous meditation, maybe making the decision to place a loved one into a care home. Having done it, I can truly say that it's probably the hardest decision that I've ever had to make in my life. Your head tells you that it's the correct move because you can't provide the level of care needed, but your heart is full of anguish and guilt, because you can't do what the person wants, which is to remain at home.

That guilty feeling never goes away. When they finally pass away you then feel guilty that you couldn't achieve the level of care to meet their last few months in the home environment. Of course, having written this, I know there are many of you who have nursed loved ones at home, with support from the MacMillan nurses, or some other brilliant organisation, but when one is dealing with issues such as dementia, the situation becomes impossible and skilled help is desperately needed.

There's nothing shameful about admitting your limitations and knowing that you needed to hand your loved one onto someone with more skill than yourself. Hopefully, it won't mean that you relinquish your responsibility towards them; it leaves you free to visit, have those painful, often guilty feelings, but knowing that for the rest of the day, you can have a normal quality of life, whatever that might mean.

Your role in this situation is to spend time finding the most appropriate home for the loved one's special needs, choosing it carefully and saying to yourself, 'If I needed this kind of support, would I be prepared to live here?' If the answer is "no", then keep looking. No one wants someone they love to be known as a bed-blocker in a hospital ward. Sadly, that often happens, because families can't cope with the issues. These problems should be spoken about long before they arise and shared among the family, not swept under the carpet, hoping that the problem will go away. People are living much longer, so for many this will be an inevitable consequence of longevity.

The problem is—how do we care as a society? It has to start by valuing our elders, seeing them as special people and respecting them. We often have the attitude of hoping the problem will go away, and leaving it for someone else to clear up. When we feel like that, we must try and focus on who they were, and what they meant to us. If it has been a good relationship in past years, that will be much easier, but if family relationships have been severely strained, or perhaps even almost non-existent, then this is a very difficult time; the sense of "payback" for the years that they have devoted towards us, may not be there, and what could come to the fore, is resentment.

So, how do we deal with it? The only way possible is that every human being has their right to take their place in the world, and if they matter to God then they should matter to us.

I know that it can be hard to love sometimes, but Christ taught about forgiving, not seven times, but seventy times seven. We should pray that we would do the same.

A thought:

There will be many elderly people who know that they are in the twilight of their years, but they have not adequately prepared for it. Some might not have made a will, or thought about the problems that not getting their house in order will leave for their children, or people close to them. Again, it's all about not sweeping things under the carpet, but realistically facing them head on. Amazingly, we all think we're going to live forever, but we never know the time, the day, or the hour, and like a good boy scout, it helps to be prepared.

We should try and broach this subject with our parents. We may have to try many times because we get a stone wall, but the answer is to never give up. It's terribly difficult to suddenly find ourselves in a parental role, taking charge of people who were once strong, and coming to terms with that, but if we give it over to God, He will see us through.

A prayer:

Lord, be with those elderly people who suddenly find themselves lonely and isolated. Give them the strength and courage still to reach out through clubs and day centres provided by people such as Age Concern or the local authority. This may not be the way they would choose to go, but it does help to ease the sense of isolation. May they find meaningful friendships and realise that their life can still have purpose, whatever age they are. Help those who are involved with their care to be kind, loving and gentle, help them to have a feeling that they are caring for a special person with special needs. Give those who care, the respect that they should have for someone older than themselves, who may have had many life-challenging experiences that can teach us so much.

May they always be given the dignity that they richly deserve. Lord, when the situation gets tough, and we feel like walking away, give us the strength to return the next day and deal with the emotional battering that we frequently experience, and not be too angry.

Bereavement

When the end comes, even though it might be expected, it's still a shock. It can also, if I'm honest, be a sense of relief that maybe the person's suffering or personal struggle is finally over. For many elderly people, the sense that they didn't have a quality of life, for several years, is something that we, as younger, fitter people, should feel sad about.

When we have the unenviable task of going through personal effects, and clearing a house, it's truly distressing. When, so often, we see how little the person leaves behind for so many years of existence. Of course, sometimes, there will always be exceptions to this rule, there will be those elderly people who may have amassed a great deal of wealth. When we see the personal possessions left behind by Mr and Mrs Average, the old saying comes to mind; 'you come in with nothing and go out with nothing,' so materialistic things do not matter, and there is no point in accruing a mass of possessions.

My husband always used to say that if you think that the contributions you have made in life are important, use the bucket of water technique to test it out. By that, he meant put your hand in a bucket of water, move it around and see how many ripples you make, and then take your hand out of the water—within seconds, it will be as though you had never placed your hand into it; you could say that that is the level of importance that you would have achieved through life. For a good many, when they leave this earth, it will be as though they never existed—very few will stay in the minds of many; it's quite a salutary thought.

The preparations for the funeral can be frantic; I can remember that I worked solidly for three weeks on my husband's funeral, and all the paperwork following the death, some of which is obvious, some of which you haven't even given a second thought to. There's a very useful booklet supplied by the Registrar's Office, which can help as a sort of "checklist" to make sure that you've carried out all the necessary tasks. Whilst you keep busy, it's fine, but when you have time to think, and be still, that's when it hits. It's never the big things that cause the pain; it's the little memories, the special piece of music that transports you into a certain situation within seconds, and you relive it, or you hear that person's voice talking to you, and sometimes you may feel their presence so strongly.

People may find this frightening, others may find it comforting. It's certainly not something to be afraid of, after all, it would be very strange if we wiped out years of somebody's presence and pretended they never existed.

The first anniversary of everything is so hard, the first birthday, wedding anniversary, Christmas, and of course, the anniversary of the death itself. But once all these have been completed, it's the passport, not to forget the loved one, but to allow yourself to begin again and concentrate on the people around you that you love, and get on with your life. Death and bereavement, difficult though they are, are just a part of the natural passing of time. Don't be frightened by them, celebrate that person's life. On dark days, try to remember the good times and the little things that the person did for you that were so special, remember them but don't get stuck in the grief. Your loved one wouldn't want you to be immobilised by grief; they would want you to cry and then move on.

There is no shame in crying—tears are cathartic. Though we think the wounds will never heal, they will eventually, but only if we are kind to ourselves. Don't beat yourself up, but try to love yourself and the life that you are still sharing, and enjoy it.

A thought:

We can't go through life without experiencing the loss of someone close to us, it's an inevitable consequence of the very life that we are given. The sudden death of someone that we know or love puts our own life in perspective; we never know when death will come.

What we know is that we only have one life, a life that God wants us to live to the full, appreciating the beauty of His world and all its abundant gifts.

Never forget to tell someone that you love them, give them a friendly hug, an arm around the shoulder, or a kindly word, because you may not get a second chance.

A prayer:

Lord, be with those today who are struggling with bereavement and feel lost and bereft because they no longer have their loved one. Help them not to feel inhibited by their emotions, help them not to hold it in when it gets too much, but help them to realise that tears are appropriate and nothing to be ashamed of. For those of us who don't know what to say when we meet someone who is bereaved, help us just to be there, to take their hand and perhaps say nothing—sometimes silence is the most appropriate action, it's not always necessary to fill the space. Help those who are grieving to be comfortable in silence and to be aware of their thoughts.

Lord, all too often, we make promises to people who are bereaved, we say that we'll keep in touch, that we won't forget, and we extend an invitation for the bereaved person to come and see us. Let those promises that we make be real and meaningful, and let us truly practice what we say we'll do and help the person along their difficult road. Lord, give the bereaved person the courage to turn up the photographs and look at them, to touch something that was important to their loved one, and rejoice in their memory.

Being a Good Neighbour

We are taught within the Christian faith to live by the Ten Commandments, one of which is 'to love your neighbour as yourself.' What do we really mean, in this day and age, about loving your neighbour as yourself? All too often, we live in a busy street, or a block of flats, where we rarely come across our neighbours, people keep themselves to themselves, for they are fearful of imposing, or being seen as "nosey"; no one wants to be labelled as a "nosey neighbour" or a "busybody". Gone are the days when people knocked on the door to borrow a cup of sugar; the shopping is now done online and delivered in bulk, so running out of something rarely happens.

The cup of sugar was often the way in; I can remember, in my childhood, that we had a neighbour who was constantly knocking on the door asking to borrow all kinds of items, from sugar to vegetables and beyond, it was her way of getting her foot in the door. Coming into the house and looking around, especially if she had seen a furniture van outside our front door! In the end, my mother used to invite her in to see the new item that we had purchased, so that she didn't have to go through all this rigmarole.

Often, we hear of incidents where elderly people have died, and lain in their property for days until they were discovered. It may have been the milkman who noticed that the milk had not been taken off the doorstep and raised the alarm, then the local neighbours felt guilty because they hadn't realised this person was ill or lonely and hadn't done anything about it.

Being a good neighbour means keeping a watchful eye, seeing the need and plugging the gap. For example, when someone has to do a lot of hospital visiting at a worrying time, being there with a casserole that they just have to put in the oven, or timing your evening meal for when they get home and inviting them to share around your kitchen table. Doing the shopping when they are too frail and ill to get out, or driving them to an important hospital appointment, perhaps being a good neighbour means getting up in the early morning and driving someone to the airport for a holiday.

Yes, you could say, 'They can get a taxi,' but how much kinder it is when they don't have the worry of wondering if the taxi will turn up on time. Being a good neighbour might mean offering to do the garden of a disabled or elderly person, rather than talking about the wilderness that their garden has become, being prepared to cut things back and hoe the weeds, simple tasks in themselves, but when your neighbour is no longer able to do them, those simple tasks to them seem as huge as climbing a mountain.

Your neighbour recognises and knows all too well what needs to be done, but if they don't have the physical ability, the finances, or the will, then the recognition means nothing. For a good neighbour to say, 'Let me help you with that,' means everything. Each time you do a kindness, you're doing it to one of God's people, whether they are believers or not. Perhaps helping a non-believer may be the very way you bring them to Christ, for it's by our deeds that we shall be known.

A thought:

If you spend your life proclaiming that you can manage, keeping people at arm's length, then what will happen is that you'll never allow them to get close to you. I can remember a time when somebody told me that they hated my guts because I had people always willing to lend a hand. This person felt on the edge of things and awkward, not knowing how to make friends, or what she should do, she was always scared of saying or doing the wrong thing, so, consequently people didn't warm to her.

When someone does something for you, even when there may be times when you don't want it done, you must accept it gracefully, otherwise, on another occasion it may not be offered. We know our good neighbours by becoming a good neighbour ourselves, reaching out in love and friendship, and being grateful for the help offered.

A prayer:

Lord, in this world of selfishness, help us to think beyond "our" needs. Help us to put others first, reaching out in love and friendship, meeting the need, whatever it might be, and being a good neighbour and thereby a good friend for years to come.

Christian Outreach

Why is it, I ask myself, that so many churches have dwindling congregations and little or no evidence of a Sunday School? Years ago, we were forced by our parents to go to church on Sunday; I know that in some instances children were sent to worship to give Mum and Dad time on their own; nevertheless, it was the means of Christian values at a very young age that one hoped would stand the test of time.

The church is much more than just a building, it's a foundation for life, and it's the cornerstone of values, standing out in a secular world. However, the church is only as good as the people in it, and if you don't have good leadership, the church will die on its feet. The Salvation Army has a very useful motto, it's 'Heart to God and Hand to Man.' The people outside church life may never have any real experience of Christianity; it says, 'By your deeds you shall be known.' We have to live Christ's teaching, for what was so impressive, was that even when he was wronged, he was still able to say, 'Father, forgive them for they know not what they do.'

By that, I mean reaching out to others in need, putting them before yourself, checking on someone, even if it's by the telephone, and listening when they have a need to spill the beans. For many it's not what you say, it's what you do. That outreach might mean transporting someone to and from hospital, giving them a meal, staying with an elderly person whilst the carer goes shopping, or staying the course during long-term illness.

It isn't about preaching the Word; it's about meeting people where they are, and making junior church vibrant and meaningful to the young, for they are the church of tomorrow.

Pastoral care is another area of the church where I feel extremely frustrated. People breeze in but don't stay the course, it's not about bringing the odd bunch of flowers, it's about being genuinely interested in the people who haven't been able to get to church, for one reason or another. Christian outreach is about bringing hope where there doesn't appear to be any, we want a nation of happy Christians. By that, I don't necessarily mean dancing in the church aisles, but we want to have a group of people who stand out from the rest, because they are absolutely sure that Christ loves them, the kind of love that makes your heart burst when the light dawns, and you feel, as well as see, that transformation.

The ministry of the church needs to get away from the lofty building and go into the marketplace, and the workplace, to prove to others that Christianity still has a presence.

When we realise that the ministry of the Christian church started with just twelve disciples, and now it has grown to millions of people throughout the world, we realise that Christianity and God's teaching, either in the home or in the workplace, starts with us. There's no other way to spread God's love than through us. A Christian home is usually a place worth visiting, where people freely share what they have, and give of themselves, so it's helpful to strive for this goal, even if we don't always achieve it.

A thought:

People have tried to modernise the church for the youth of today, by using pop music, guitars and other modern keyboards, etc. Perhaps this is where we're going wrong, because it's a forced modernisation, and in some cases, a forced hope. What should happen is that people find what they are searching for, through the teaching of the Bible, and through the ministering of the Word. This has to be done in such a way that it's relevant in today's world.

One thing I'm sure of is that all the disturbances around the world that we see on our televisions, show us that modern day values are not always working. By and large, we want a get-rich-quick society and there's a division between those who have and those who don't, and this makes for an unfair, disgruntled society.

The emphasis on Christ's teaching was one of love and respect and kindness and helpfulness to others; this is where we seem to have gone wrong, because now we live in a world where it's just looking after number one, and, I feel, we would be a much happier society if we looked towards another human being to see where help can be given. I'm sure it's worth going back to the basics, and looking at the Ten Commandments, in particular—which is a charter for life.

A prayer:

Lord, don't let the church be just on the high street, but in the hearts and minds of every human being. Let the love that Christ taught us be truly shared, one to another, in unconditional love. Let the church be a place of welcome, a place of refuge, a place where we can be free to express our feelings, and more importantly, let it be a place of love. Let the values of church life be transferred into family life, and let us always give time to those we love, and those we find difficult to love.

Spiritual Development at Any Age

We never know when God will speak to us; it can be in a crowded street, the workplace, countryside, a church service, or at any difficult period in our life, or even more importantly, a time of great happiness. Often, when life is tough, we don't hear God's voice, we feel completely abandoned, but it has been my experience that when God calls and you answer, it's a bit like the feeling you have when you find true love for the first time. There's an overwhelming joy, yet there's also confusion, you realise that you're on the edge of something that will change your life forever.

When I met my husband Ralph, he was a confessed atheist, but this God of ours has a sense of humour, he put him with a Methodist local preacher. How ironic is that? I knew that banging on about God would serve no purpose, my husband had to find his own path, yet, hopefully, I'd be there to share it with him. Four-and-a half-years on into our marriage, one thing was for sure, and that was, that when he committed to Christ, his life would change. When that happens you're often the butt, and sometimes the ridicule, of people's comments, they find it strange that someone in middle age can find God, but that's a wonderful thing about the Christian faith.

When we stop refusing to allow the door to open, and allow God in, it can be an amazing moment of revelation, a light suddenly dawning. There's no doubt that when we know Christ as part of our life we look at the world in a different way, we see people in a different light, we look for the best, and we try to live our life in the way that God would expect us to. Living by the standards of the Ten Commandments is a pretty good yardstick.

If, for example, we loved our neighbour as ourselves, and we put God first, and other people first, before exercising our own needs, this world would be a much happier place. I can remember Ralph saying, when people asked why he had made the decision to ask Christ to come into his life, that he realised that, I had something that he wanted to be a part of, he didn't want to be on the outside looking in.

Before he gave his life to Christ he was only interested in, as he put it, "me and mine". Now, because he tried to live in the way that God expected, he realised that he had to become other-centred. Our house was an ever-open door; weekends were a time when we always had someone sitting at our table—often, someone who was lonely, and had no one to share their day with. It was pastoral care in the true sense. We helped people whose marriages had broken down, and they needed a place to stay, or time to have a shower and a meal and unburden their heart. We were there sharing in a Christian ministry, and doing what we knew God expected of us— walking the walk, not talking the talk, and living by the deed, a good deed of Christian love.

By that I don't just mean that the Christian faith is one where we spend our life chasing around doing "good deeds" for others. That's a necessary part of it, of course, but sometimes it's just as important to be still, and to be quiet, and to listen or, perhaps, if the situation is traumatic, to say nothing at all, just being alongside that person, sharing in their problem. And giving them love, concern, respect and care. All through the Christian gospel we can see that Jesus showed love and respect to all whom he met, even those that made him angry, like the moneychangers in the temple, and the people selling their wares on a holy day. He taught respect by his actions and principles in the way that he taught others about living the faith.

It's very hard with all the demands that are made in a modern world to be old-fashioned, in some people's eyes, standing up for what you believe in, and to speak up for what you know. Yet, have the courage to do that, although we must not be over zealous with our enthusiasm, because sometimes that can put people off. What we need to do, is love them into the Kingdom of God by our thoughts and kindness, not by Bible-thumping. How we are seen by the wider public is the embodiment of the Christian faith.

A thought:

There will be those who will laugh, and say, 'What, at your age? What's the matter with you?' But, if we have the courage to stand up and be counted, and talk about why we turn to Christ in middle age, or whatever age it might happen to be, then we may well bring people to God in the best possible way. We live, sadly, in an extremely selfish world, it's every man for himself, dog eat dog. But the Christian faith teaches that we must sacrifice ourselves to help others, that will be a totally new concept to some people.

The Christian faith doesn't mean that we have a "get rich quick" mentality on the back of other people. It should mean that we live a life of integrity, a life where we try to express love, kindness and gentleness to others. If that means that we come across to some individuals as being too consistently nice then so be it. What a privilege to have that written on your tombstone, for it will mean that you lived an exemplary life and there's no finer memorial than that.

A prayer:

Lord, when someone turns away from their old lifestyle, and they turn to You for a new beginning, help them to reach out in faith, help them to trust You, to know that You'll be there, whatever challenges may beset them in life. Help them to have a zest for knowledge, to read and understand, and gain comfort from Your Word. Help them when they find it hard to pray, words often don't come easy in a busy world, it's difficult to find space, and quiet, with mobile phones and other electronic gadgetry getting in the way.

Help them to find a place of stillness, where they can rest in You, and find You, let it be a father and child relationship between You, Lord, and us the children, and that they know that You'll be there guiding and comforting in the years ahead.

Celebration

If we look back on our life, it's the things that we celebrated that seem to stick in our minds. They are necessary to counteract the boring day-to-day things that go on. Celebrations lift our spirit, create happiness and make us feel good. They are a time when we can let our hair down, shout and whoop for joy and be childishly excited. The whole point of celebration is that we take our friends with us. We don't normally celebrate by ourselves, it's a time of togetherness, a time of completeness, and a time when we want our friends and family to be joyous with us, and for us.

It's a fantastic feeling when, just for that one special moment, you throw caution to the wind, making that day very special. We've plenty of time to be serious and watch the pennies; this is the time for saying what the heck...

When that invitation lands on our doormat, often the first emotion that we feel is one of gladness for the fact that we have been included in this great occasion. The gift that we bring is an expression of our love for that person, a sense in which we want to share in their joy and enthusiasm. Perhaps the most important aspect is the sense of togetherness and belonging, the sense of being included, which makes the whole thing wonderful.

This party has to be something that the person will remember for the rest of their life, it's a landmark, or signpost, on life's road.

None of us know what will happen in life, opportunities for celebration come all too infrequently, so we have to grab the moment and make the most of it. That doesn't mean that we have to end up completely legless in an alcoholic stupor, although I know that is how some people like to celebrate, but it does mean that we should make the most of every God-given moment.

A thought:

It's fantastic to have events to celebrate. A life without celebration is a life without meaning. It's also a life that can often be bereft of friendship, and that's perhaps the saddest thought of all. We must take every opportunity to be joyous, to thank God for the life that we have been given, a life that, if we share it with others, can be enriching and fulfilling.

A prayer:

Lord, as we think of the opportunity to celebrate, help us remember the precious gift that You gave us in Jesus Christ, the precious gift of Your Son, given to us. Help us celebrate the life that You've given in service and gratitude, and help us have a life that's full of thankfulness for every God-given day.

Also by this author:

Undefeated by Lin Berwick, published by Epworth Press 1980

Inner Vision by Lin Berwick published by Arthur James Limited 1990—Now out of print

God's Rich Pattern by Dr Lin Berwick MBE published by SPCK 2012

On the Count of Three by Dr Lin Berwick MBE published by Kindle Direct Publishers 2022

Nobody Does It Better Than Me: The Story of Alma by Dr Lin Berwick MBE published by Austin Maccauley Publishers in 2023.